MAYA LAND
IN COLOR

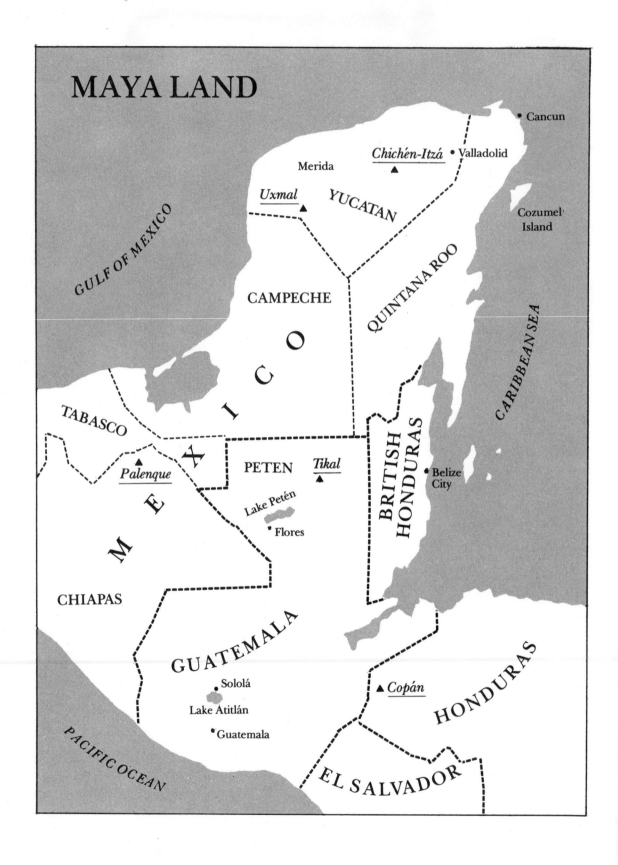

MAYA LAND
in Color

Text and Photographs by
WALTER R. AGUIAR

HASTINGS HOUSE · PUBLISHERS
New York 10016

PUBLISHED 1978 BY HASTINGS HOUSE, PUBLISHERS, INC.

Library of Congress Cataloging in Publication Data
Aguiar, Walter R.
   Maya land in color.

   (Profiles of America)
   1. Mayas—Antiquities. 2. Mexico—
Antiquities. 3. Central America—Antiquities.
4. Mexico—Description and travel—1951–
—Guide-books. 5. Central America—Description
and travel—1951– —Guide-books. I. Title.
F1435.A56 972 78-2537
ISBN 0-8038-4703-3

Published simultaneously in Canada by
Saunders of Toronto, Ltd., Don Mills, Ontario

Printed and bound in Hong Kong by Mandarin Publishers Limited

CONTENTS

Maya Land

WHO WERE the Mayas? Where did they come from? This has been, and still is, a subject of deep controversy. There are many theories afloat, in limbo between fact and fiction. I want to give the reader a clear and easy interpretation of the true findings recorded up to the present—or at least those that offer a more logical interpretation.

Only further studies and archaeological findings in new sites will give positive answers. Perhaps hundreds or even thousands of ancient monuments still exist, abandoned by unknown builders for unknown reasons, and remain jealously guarded by the jungle growth. What answers lie in the secret places of these temples and pyramids? Someday, somewhere may be found more of the precious codices and hieroglyphic writings which the Spanish conquerors, influenced by fanatically "anti-pagan" priests, tried to exterminate. From the findings in the interior of the Temple of the Inscriptions in Palenque in 1952 and many others found throughout Tikal and Chichén-Itzá we can be confident of future discoveries and clues to unveil more of the secrets of this splendid civilization.

What you will see through my photographs is only an introduction to what you will experience when you travel to these remains of one of the most impressive and extraordinary cultures of the past.

The First Colonization

STILL A THEORY, but one of the strongest thus far, is that the initial colonization of the New World was accomplished by peoples from Asia who crossed the Bering Straits land bridge until the Pleistocene, or Ice Age, and that by the year 9,000 B.C. most of the Americas were already inhabited by these early men. The Bering Straits land bridge disappeared when the waters of the sea rose to approximately 400 feet during the deglaciation period, about 10,000 B.C. According to recent findings, the ancestral Maya were already living in the area of the Chiapas-Guatemala highlands by 2,500 B.C.

An obsidian projectile point said to be from the Clovis people—who inhabited Alaska, Canada and the United States some ten to twelve thousand years ago—has been found in Guatemala. Archaeologists have been able to determine from materials found in these areas, after all carbon tests were performed, that these people comprised the first culture that existed in the Americas. This obsidian point is the earliest artifact to be found to date in Maya country. It is possible that these people brought, or introduced, maize and other cultivables to the area.

Visitors from the Other Continents

THERE ARE many pieces of evidence supporting the belief that people from other cultures visited America long before Columbus in 1492, including Phoenicians and Vikings. There are similarities between the style and features of pottery discovered in many parts of the Americas and that of cultures of the Old World.

One clay figure with an astonishing resemblance to that of a Viking was unearthed from the Chan-Chan ruins in Trujillo, Perú, the birthplace of the pre-Columbian Chimú culture. The figure shows a pointed beard and long clothing used by the Vikings—features that the Chimú civilization did not have.

Reed fishing boats used by fishermen on Lake Chad in Africa are similar to those from Lake Titicaca in Perú. The Chimú people of Perú also used reed boats for fishing along the coast of the Pacific, where local people, presumably their descendants, still use the same construction techniques as their ancestors. The Chimú boats differ from those of Lake Titicaca in that they are built to carry only one person. These reed boats of Huanchaco are called "caballitos"—little horses.

Chinese records are reported to show that around 500 A.D. a Chinese Buddhist monk, Jwui Shan, and five companions, all Buddhist missionaries, voyaged to the Americas. Sailing down the coast of California to Mexico and perhaps Central America, they spent some time in this region, which might account for the presence of Indians in Mexico with much accentuated Oriental features. The stelae in Copán that are carved with human figures bear Chinese features, and some of the accounts of the Chinese voyage show that the travelers found a civilized people who knew writing done on paper made from a plant, and possessed silver and gold.

Bitter controversies have arisen concerning the extent to which the influence of a culture has spread to different regions, especially in the case of those far distant from each other and before recorded history. Experts have demonstrated that such contacts were possible, by considering ocean currents as well as the seaworthiness of ancient crafts. The RA II, a reconstruction of an ancient Egyptian reed boat, with the Norwegian anthropologist-explorer Thor Heyerdahl as captain, has dramatically proved the possibility of early unrecorded contacts.

If such contacts occurred, they were isolated events, for the visitors did not influence the cultural developments of the pre-Columbian peoples. For example, these people neither invented nor borrowed through introduction, the wheel as a means of transportation, except on toys, nor the potter's wheel, the spinning wheel, or the rotary *quern* (hand mill). Nor did these pre-Columbian people know or use the plow in their agriculture; they developed agriculture without this technique.

But by contrast, they built beautiful cities, ruled over vast empires, created dramatic works of art—with remarkably unique skill.

Recorded History

THE MAYAS OF pre-Columbian America were the only culture to evolve a highly developed hieroglyphic writing system on stone and on paper which they transformed into books. This system was so complex that when attempts were made to decipher it, it was beyond any comprehensive point of departure: each glyph had a signification. Most were deciphered, but many of them still withhold so much information that Maya studies are a continuous challenge to modern archaeologists.

Even more pictorial and expressive than those of the early Egyptians, the hieroglyphs show no influence from the outside world, though it is still possible that the idea of picture-writing could have been transmitted to the New World by cultures from the Old. Opinions are divided.

At the time of the Spanish arrival on the Yucatán peninsula in the 1500's, the Mayas were already a vanishing civilization, but they had recorded the extraordinary events of their past in books, which they consulted for the worship of their gods. These books were made of tree-bark paper folded and bound in a pair of wooden covers, as well as of deer skin rolled as scrolls.

The Church of Mérida, headed by Diego de Landa, was so eager to remove once and for all any traces of non-Christian worship that it destroyed all the priceless manuscripts it could find. In a huge fire made deliberately at the center of the plaza of

Maní, Landa supervised the burning of 5,000 idols, 13 huge stones, presumably altars, 22 smaller stones, 27 Maya books written on deerskin and some 200 painted vases depicting Maya life. Fortunately, after this display of hostility to the Maya religion, many books were secretly guarded and later found by the Mayas and put in safer places.

But not for long—Fray Diego was still looking for them. And who was Fray Diego? He was a Spanish priest, born 1524 and died 1579, who arrived with the conquistadors and was later made the second Bishop of Yucatán. He was the mastermind of the campaign against the Maya religion, determined to wipe out the native beliefs and literature as works of evil.

Only four codices, original Maya manuscripts, are now known to the world: The *Madrid Codex*, the *Dresden Codex* and the *Paris Codex*, are named after the cities where they are now kept. The "Troaño" Codex was found by Abbé Brasseur de Bourbourg in 1864, and when the Spanish Government discovered that it was part of the "Cortesianus" Codex in their files, it was also acquired. Together with the "Cortesianus", bought in 1875 by the Spanish Government, it is now known as the *Madrid Codex*.

The *Dresden Codex* was found in Dresden's Royal Library, where it had been kept as a "worthless souvenir." Unfortunately, this oldest and best executed codex was damaged during World War II.

The *Paris Codex*, found by Leon de Rosny in 1860, had also been misplaced, and so Rosny and Bourbourg were the heroes and discoverers of the new Maya world.

A fourth, presumably authentic, Codex, which I shall call the Mexico City Codex, surfaced in June 1971 in New York City at the Grolier Club, where it was exhibited. Its owner wished to remain anonymous, and keep to himself all information about its origin. But in December 1977 it was disclosed in the New York Times that Dr. Josué Sáenz, a former Mexican Cabinet Minister and president of the Olympics Committee, was the owner. He has donated this Codex to the Museum of Anthropology of Mexico City. It is still unclear where the Codex was found. This Codex is a sequence of hieroglyphic and pictorial passages of celestial studies of the planet Venus. It is eleven pages long and part of an original twenty-page manuscript. Dr. Michael Coe, a Yale University archaeologist who supervised the preparations for the exhibit at the Grolier Club, stated that before the Codex left the country he detached about a square inch of blank bark fiber paper for isotope-testing, confirming afterwards its 13th-century date. This new discovery is one of the most important of the Maya world in recent years.

As to the time of composition or the origin of the three other Maya manuscripts, there is no definite knowledge, because it is hazardous to treat these relics to discover their dates—these irreplaceable items might be destroyed!

Fray Diego de Landa's persecutions against the Maya past and contemporary customs were so obvious and open that he was called back to Madrid to face charges.

Brought before a panel of seven Franciscans, they exonerated him, but he spent some eight years in Spain in semi-seclusion, writing his *Relación de las Cosas de Yucatán*. He finished the book in 1566, and returned to Yucatán in 1573 as the second Bishop, staying in Mérida until his death in 1579.

Has he paid for the crime of destroying such valuable records of a vanished culture? Possibly, for in spite of all his efforts to obliterate the Maya past, he was the first eminent scholar to help preserve their customs. He gave to the world of archaeology a wealth of information that has been consulted by scholars and researchers. His work has helped in deciphering many archaeological findings.

Fray Diego's original manuscript was lost and copies remained forgotten in the archives of the Spanish Royal Academy, with many other post-Conquest records. It was in the dark almost three hundred years until the always curious Abbé Brasseur de Bourbourg discovered it in 1863. It was translated into French, published in 1864, and much later, in 1937 it was translated into English.

Science and Technology

THE MAYAS showed remarkable similarities to the early civilizations of the Nile and Euphrates basins. They learned controlled agriculture; they were pyramid builders, astronomers, calendar makers; and they developed their own form of a written language. These were astonishing achievements for a simple farming people living in a tropical environment of fast-growing jungle and swamps.

They used stone tools only. Their knowledge of metal was introduced at a later date, presumably through trade from Costa Rica, but included only gold and some pieces of copper, which they used for ornamental and ceremonial purposes only.

The writing system developed by the Mayas, considered one of the most complex in the New World, is composed of hieroglyphs representing their mythological beliefs, carved in stelae and on temples. These records may be of important events—or simply descriptions of their daily life. How they perfected their writing methods is not clear. There are no signs of any early transitional materials used to reach, step by step, such an advanced system of carving and writing. They may have begun by using wooden tablets, rawhide scrolls and other very perishable materials.

Maya farmers cleared the land by burning, leaving the ashes as fertilizer, a method still used. They made holes for seed corn with pointed sticks, and food crops such as sweet potatoes, peppers and tomatoes were grown. They wove cloth from cotton and dyed it in bright colors.

Their dependence on the harvest was so great that they studied the moon, sun and stars in order to tell accurate time and predict the planting as well as the season for the rains. Their lives were so dependent on these studies that their religion was very much related to the movement of heavenly bodies. To build their temples and monuments, the Mayas, refined builders that they were, cut blocks of limestone. They also learned to make bricks and to use mortar and stucco. But they never achieved a true arch in their buildings. These buildings were impressively massive and solid in appearance but were decorated with intricate carvings, elaborately carved pillars of stone, and stairways. Though dated hieroglyphs have provided scholars and researchers with fascinating material, much of it remains a mystery.

The Maya technique in transporting stone for building and other purposes was to use logrollers. The stone was then fitted in place by grinding and chiseling with stone and obsidian tools, which were also used for carving and in human sacrifices. Obsidian was used by them the way we use metal—they depended on it and accomplished so much that they did not see the need for anything new. Roads or causeways and plazas were paved with flagstones, and limestone gravel was distributed on top and then pulverized with enormous stone rollers. One of these was found in the vicinity of Quintana Roo in Mexico.

Mesoamerican Pyramids

THE PYRAMID had the highest religious significance for the Mayas and other cultures of Mesoamerica. According to recent findings, the pyramid had also a funerary function, though this needs more clarification. Throughout Mexico the burial custom of many cultures seems to have been cremation or simple burials, with some exceptions. The Zapotecs, a culture occupying Monte Albán, had an elaborate burial site, Mitla, the sacred city, which means "Place of the Dead." People buried here, the center for these ritual ceremonies or at any other designated buildings were evidently of high rank.

Every pyramid found in Mesoamerica has been in steps, usually so high as to be precarious to climb, especially to descend, and none of the stairways had balustrades or handrails.

Some pyramids had stairs on all sides, like El Castillo in Chichén-Itzá. The Temple of the Magician in Uxmal has two stairways on opposite sides, but most were usually on the front. At the top of each pyramid was a temple with crests, some of which rose fifty feet over the temples, as in Temple V at Tikal. Although their function is not clear, the erection of such high crests was of apparently great importance to the Maya.

The façades and their ornamentation at Uxmal, and the urban composition at Tikal, Palenque, Chichén-Itzá and Copán are of overwhelming beauty. The Maya architect gave great importance to the proper placement of the buildings, too, as if each one were facing a certain constellation. Bishop de Landa was so impressed with the Maya architecture that he wrote, "...so many in so many places and so well built of stone are they; it is a marvel; the buildings themselves and their number are the most outstanding thing that has been discovered in the Indies."

The Calendar and Maya Mathematics

THE CALENDAR was one of the greatest inventions of the Mayas. It was developed by the astronomer-priests in charge of studying the sun, moon, and stars in their attempts to understand the gods. They, like the Egyptians, counted days, and also like them, computed the year. The Maya round calendar, based on solar observation, was called HAAB, and consisted of 20 months of 18 days each, with one additional month of 5 days. This extra month was called UAYEB. The calendar totaled 365 days and was as accurate as the calendar we use today. While the Egyptians were inclined to believe in chronological time as an ordered sequence, the Maya were busy with arithmetic oddities. They thought of time as composed of overlapping cycles of divine numbers which they worshipped in connection with the harvest. Their gods were those of the sun, rain, soil, and corn. Among others, there was a moon goddess.

The Maya calendar of around 600 A.D. was far more accurate than the Gregorian calendar adopted in Europe in the 1500's. Maya astronomers, without any optical devices, could follow the movements of planets and stars and accurately predict eclipses. They recorded these events in their calendars. This extraordinary system is practically impossible to explain in simple terms, but the Mayas must have pursued complexity because they enjoyed it. To understand the Maya adoration for calculation, consider that they were often involved in computations corresponding to that of ascertaining on what day of the week the 31st of December 90,000,000 B.C. would fall! Imagine the mental efforts of the Maya priests keeping track of time through complex astronomy and the physical burden of the laborers erecting such a majestic compound of buildings without the use of the wheel and metal!

Their superior mathematical concepts were one of the Maya's greatest achievements. They were already using the zero in the third century A.D., though it was not in use in Spain until the seventh century, where it had been introduced by the Arabs but was not officially used until the fifteenth century.

The Mayan numerical writing system

OUR present Gregorian calendar considers the solar year to be 365.2425 days, allowing one Leap Year every four years, with the exception of a century year, which becomes a Leap Year only when divided by four hundred. Based on the sidereal year system calculated by astronomy, scientists consider the total length of the year as 365.2420 days, while the account of Maya calculations was the same!

———	BAR	=	5
• • • •	4 dots	=	4
• • •	3 dots	=	3
• •	2 dots	=	2
•	1 dot	=	1
⬯	Zero		

They used bars and dots to write all numbers less than 20

$\overset{\bullet}{=} = 6$ $\overset{\bullet\bullet}{=} = 7$ $\overset{\bullet\bullet\bullet}{=} = 8$ $\overset{\bullet\bullet\bullet\bullet}{=} = 9$

$= 10$ $= 11$ $= 12$ $= 13$

$= 14$ $= 15$ $= 16$ $= 17$

$= 18$ $= 19$ etc.

365.2420 days, while the account of Maya calculations was the same!

The Mayas recorded the passage of time and events on practically everything they created, but carved stelae found in so many centers as to reveal a kind of "stela cult", were a favorite monument to register in glyph form the important happenings that affected their lives. The stelae, with their location recorded along with the events depicted on them, were erected every twenty years, it is believed, but in the Maya decline they were built every ten, and then every five until their construction completely stopped.

The earliest calendar "Long Count" date, equated to 292 A.D., from the Maya lowlands, was discovered on Stela No. 29, now at the Tikal Museum. The "Long Count" system was an extremely accurate method of measuring time; it was based on a 52-year cycle and is correct up to within a few hours. This "Long Count" system was abandoned long before the conquest. The Maya ceremonial calendar, TZOLKIN, based on celestial studies, has an error of only a single day in 6,000 years—in contrast our Gregorian calendar has a one-day error every four years, which becomes a leap year.

Social Organization

MANY MAGNIFICENT monuments have been found broken and scattered among the ruins that have been explored, and buildings have been found whose construction was halted in the middle. Perhaps priests and lords were assassinated by mobs, who might have looted and destroyed parts of their monuments and stelae. Perhaps the ruling class was pressed by high priests inspired by an unknown force. This ruling class may have in turn demanded more and more, including the never-ending tributes and sacrifices, from the common inhabitants of these cities. The people may have finally rebelled against their "divine masters," who had been driven to such a tyrannical state.

The masses were not permitted to acquire any knowledge of, or participate in, the priests' studies in astronomy, mathematics, and philosophy. Only selected persons would be trained to succeed them, and to continue their scientific studies. The high priests, through the lords of the ruling class, were the absolute masters of the Maya population, and their reign continued through the Golden Era—the Classic Era—of the Maya civilization, in which it reached its maximum of knowledge in science and mathematics.

The second in rank and power were the nobility, who handled government affairs. In this organized system of leadership, the lords were in charge of government with second-ranked lords assisting the head of government. The officials next in rank acted as councilors and minor deputies who carried out orders from their superiors.

Women were occupied with housekeeping, cooking, weaving their colorful cotton cloth, and caring for the children. Farming and manual labor for the high priests and lords were done by the men. They fired the land to clear it for farming, then planted red and black beans, squash, melons, tomatoes, sweet potatoes, and their most important vegetable, the sacred corn, or maize. When the farming season was over, the people had other tasks that were organized and supervised by the upper class. There were always community projects like constructing temples, roads and causeways, or making carvings....

Each settlement was served by a medicine man who would call on the sick to prescribe a combination of medicinal herbs or whatever circumstances required and the doctor's experience indicated. The parts that caused pain were often bled. If the victim died, the corpse was cremated or buried underneath the floor of the house, which was commonly abandoned afterward by the surviving members of the family.

Musical instruments were part of the Maya religious festivities and played an important role in their lives. The instruments included whistles, ocarinas, flutes, drums, rattles, conch-shell trumpets, and turtle-carapace drums.

The Maya ritual feasts, which were ruled by the religious calendar, the TZOLKIN calendar, were in adoration of their gods, each of which had a specific function. Hunab Kú, the creator of all things, was in turn father of Itzamna, god of the heavens and of day and night. Kukúlkán, god of the wind, was also known as Quetzalcoatl, the feathered serpent god. Chac was the god of rain and Yum Kaax the young god of corn. Ek Chuah was the patron of merchants and Ix Tab the god of suicides. Ix Chel was the moon goddess, Ix Asal Uo, the patroness of weaving, and Ah Puch the god of death.

The common people were the ones who had to bear the heaviest burden in their communities, though they seem to have endured it well. The lords, not the priests, ruled and decided on the future of the masses. When victims for a sacrifice were needed, they raided towns in nearby communities in search of captives. In Maya paintings and stone sculptures are depicted rituals including torture, heart removal and decapitation. One of the largest administrative capitals and ceremonial centers was Tikal. The lords lived close to the high priests in communal palatial quarters.

Decline of a Civilization

THE REASONS FOR the decline of the Maya culture are not known. About 900 A.D., at the peak of their achievements in science, art and architecture, the Classic Period, they no longer devised a calendar or built their temples. In some places they stopped all activity as early as A.D. 800-810. It is hard to believe that the high priests, armed with the tremendous power of the knowledge they possessed, and supported by the lords and other classes in complete command of the masses, could have permitted any rebellion.

Scientists speculate that a natural disaster occurred, perhaps an epidemic or a drought or even the erosion of the soil, which could no longer produce the crops necessary for survival. But there is no proof. Did the people rebel against their leaders, a ruthless priestly hierarchy? In my opinion, this is one of the most logical theories.

The last stronghold of the Maya was Chichén-Itzá, which at a later date was invaded by the Toltecs who imposed their strong militaristic domination. This latter Maya-Toltec era lasted from the tenth to the late thirteenth century. Yucatán was officially discovered when Hernandez de Córdoba, from Cortés' army, landed in Cabo Catoche in 1517. Córdoba met with a violent reception from the Mayas there in the province of Ecab. The Mayas at the time were politically disoriented and their ambitions were diminished, but what would have happened if Hernandez de Córdoba had arrived at the peak of their capabilities?

He later commented that his army overpowered the Maya only because of the advantage of firearms. The Maya were still very well organized, and as long as their culture lasted they were able to urbanize such large towns as Tikal, Copán, Palenque, Uxmal and Chichén-Itzá, and others. Remains of public baths have been found at Chichén-Itzá, reservoirs at Tikal, and observation towers at Palenque and Chichén-Itzá.

John Lloyd Stephens, Explorer from the United States

IF STEPHENS and his companion, Frederick Catherwood, were to revisit many of the Maya ruins they explored in 1839 and 1840, their eyes would delight in the new look of these magnificent Maya cities and the extraordinary restoration of temples, pyramids and their surroundings. From all over the world tourists come to the Yucatán peninsula, a limestone platform of 80,000 square miles, to visit Chichén-Itzá, Uxmal, Palenque, and many other sites in Mexico—and Tikal in Guatemala and Copán in Honduras. New roads are being built and other sites are being cleared and restored, to make this area a wonderland for all interested in the Maya culture.

J. L. Stephens was born in Shrewsbury, New Jersey in 1805. His accounts of his explorations in the company of the English architect Frederick Catherwood, who was assigned by his commander and friend to draw the archaeological sites, through the many Maya ruins in Mesoamerica in 1839, and Yucatán revisited in 1840—are unforgettable, especially when you have photographed all these places, as I have. The description of the ruins and temples, stelae and other monuments, as he saw them, and Catherwood's drawings, are astonishingly accurate, many just as you will see them today. The experiences of the two men as they reached all these sites, their suffering, hunger, sickness, and the like are almost unbelievable. All this for the sake of archaeology.

COPÁN

THE COPÁN RUINS and all the adjacent land were purchased by Stephens in 1839 for fifty U.S. dollars, to the delight of the landowner, to whom the ruins seemed worthless. Stephens' first glimpse gave him a surprise: "America, say historians, was peopled by savages, but savages never reared these structures, savages never carved these stones...," he commented after inspecting the four-sided stelae and other buildings at the tree-grown site. The Hieroglyphic Stairway was covered by soil and Stephens did not see it, but many years later the large mound was uncovered with the help of the Peabody Museum of Harvard, along with other buildings of the site.

The position of the buildings at this site proves that this was an astronomical observation center by the relationship to a constant observation of the sun. The building of Copán, the southernmost important Classic Maya site, began about 436 A.D. Its last monument was raised about 810 A.D. As part of their complex mathematical methods of measuring time, almost an obsession, the Mayas were obliged to erect a stela every KATUN—every 7,200 days, or 20 years. Many intricate carvings, balanced art patterns and calendars were found on these stelae.

The Maya carvings of humans and animals in their system of writing is an example of these people's sensitivity. Their work remains so faithfully realistic in anatomical proportions that anyone can easily understand and admire it.

At the end of the Maya period in Copán, it is reported that stelae were built every ten and five years consecutively. Why the rush to build stelae? Did they know that their end was nearing? Were there any changes in the measurements of time? Any constellation changes, weather changes, earthquakes, strange forces or any other reason unknown to us? We hope archaeologists will learn more about Maya writings, to unveil these mysteries.

Copán was an acropolis covering about 12 acres, which in turn overlaid an earlier village with a dwelling system common to many, if not all, Maya cities. The city was built near the Copán river, whose course was altered to save further erosion of the rear of the East Court of the North Acropolis. The city has five or more plazas, courts and pyramids, in decay, but you may see the Stairway of the Hieroglyphs, beautiful four-sided carved stelae and altars, enormous stone heads and the Serpent God at the West Court. The visitor will delight in discovering many interesting details by himself, for we all have some of that genius and sensitivity to see things in our own way no matter how skillfully they are described by others.

Will you feel as Stephens did?

"It is impossible to describe the interest with which I explored these ruins...we followed our guide, who, sometimes missing his way, with a constant and vigorous use of his machete conducted us through the thick forest, among half-buried fragments, to fourteen more monuments ('stelae') of the same character and appearance, some with more elegant designs, and some in workmanship equal to the finest monuments of the Egyptians."

The North Acropolis, containing some of the most important structures in Copán, was much the same in 1839 as today, though the forest has been cleared and loose stones put in place. Can you tell any difference between what you see and what Stephens described?

"When the machete had cleared the way, we saw that it was a square with steps on all the sides almost as perfect as those of a Roman ampitheatre. The steps were ornamented with sculpture, and one the south side, about halfway up, forced out of its place by roots, was a colossal head, again evidently a portrait."

Copán lies in one of Central America's most fertile valleys. It is 12 km long and some 3 km wide at its broadest point. In spite of its situation in the tropics, the climate of Copán is temperate and healthful, with an altitude of 2,000 feet above sea level. The dry season is from December to May; the temperature never rises above 100°F, with a usual range of from 60 to 90 degrees—it might drop below 50 at night.

Founded about 1870, the city was built on the remains of one of the Copán ruins. The entire valley shows evidence of a large pre-Columbian occupation lasting many centuries. A letter of March 8th, 1576 by Licenciado Doctor Don Diego Garcia de Palacio, a judge of the high court in Guatemala to King Philip II of Spain was the first written account of these extraordinary ruins. Don Diego mentions the superb buildings, doubting the natives of the region could have had anything to do with it, for the splendor and the skill employed were overwhelming.

The Chronicles of the Kingdom of Guatemala, written in 1700 by Francisco de Fuentes, was the first printed account. From then on there is nothing, but in 1836 Colonel Galindo, an Irishman whose real name was John Gallagher, explored these ruins under a commission from the Central American Government. His accounts were published in the proceedings of the *Royal Geographical Society of Paris* and the *Literary Gazette* of London. Stephens said Gallagher was the only one "who has ever presented Copán to the consideration of Europe and our country..." Perhaps the official discoverer of Copán was García de Palacio, but Stephens' description calls to mind the zenith of Maya culture and "the reader may imagine the effect when the whole country was clear of forest, and priest and people ascending from the outside to the terraces and thense to the holy places within to pay their adoration in the temple...."

Copán was made a National Park.

PALENQUE

FRAY RAMÓN DE ORDOÑEZ Y AGUIAR, who in 1773 was the Canon of the Cathedral of Ciudad Real de Chiapas, was one of the first explorers of Palenque. He traveled through the jungle from Chiapas to Palenque assisted by some Indians he recruited in Chiapas. He was carried on a primitive palanquin he had ordered. In 1784 Fray Aguiar completed a short essay of 23 pages on the ruins. It is not known what the Mayas called this city; the neighboring natives call it Casas de Piedras—"stone houses." Palenque is a Spanish word meaning "palisade," and its name comes from the nearby village of Santo Domingo del Palenque.

The site the Mayas chose to build Palenque is 1,000 feet above sea level, is rich in natural resources, and protected by the Chiapas mountain range and by high hills toward the Tabasco plains. It lies in the midst of hills and mountains which protect it like a fortress.

Archaeological findings confirm that Palenque has been inhabited since before the Christian era. The increasing infiltration of other cultures from the Gulf during the Late Classic Period evidently precipitated its abandonment. The site may have been occupied since then by peoples from the Gulf or the extensive surrounding dwellings. When the elite was vanquished, however, Palenque's glory ended.

In 1787 Antonio del Rio was in charge of the third expedition to Palenque. The King of Spain, Charles III, who had heard of its existence through Fray Aguiar, ordered Del Rio to send him samples of the remaining works of art. This contributed to the further deterioration of Palenque, as richly carved slabs, stucco fragments and other "samples" were shipped to Madrid. Some of these pieces survived and are now in the Museo America de Madrid.

Del Rio's findings were published in London in 1822, alerting the world to the existence of Palenque and confirming the importance of this site for Humboldt, whose work *Vue des Cordillières, et Monuments des Peuples Indigenes de L'Amerique*, published in 1816, was the first to illustrate a design based on a bas-relief sculpture from Palenque. Others followed, and each must have wanted to take home "some souvenirs." By 1832-1833, Jean Frederick Waldeck, a self-designated "Count", lived in one of the structures which was named after him, the "Temple of the Count."

Waldeck sketched many of Palenque's bas-relief sculptures to be included in *Monuments Anciens du Mexique, Palenque et Autres Ruins de l'Ancienne Civilisation du Mexique*, which he wrote in collaboration with Abbé Charles Etienne Brasseur de Bourbourg, already an authority on Maya antiquities. This work is still acclaimed, though some of the 36 drawings are part of his imagination, for we now know some of the characters to be non-existent. Many of his drawings are the only recorded source of vanished carvings.

Stephens was intrigued, and not to be outdone, he journeyed with the artist Catherwood on a voyage of one thousand miles from Copán, through jungle, mountains, and treacherous terrain, rivers—fighting the elements and the mosquitoes. Although suffering illness, the two men inspected the buildings at Palenque—Catherwood executing his drawings with an expertise that has never been surpassed. Stephens' work *Incidents of Travel in Central America: Chiapas and Yucatan,* and Catherwood's drawings, added further to the fame of Palenque.

One of Stephens' keen observations was that "the hieroglyphics are the same as those found at Copán and Quirigua," the latter of which he also visited in Guatemala. An unexpected and welcome revelation for Stephens and Catherwood was the architectural design, and the superb carvings and stucco bas-relief figures inside some of the temples. The artistry of the master craftsmen expressed in the carvings is highly individual. The figures, so perfect in their fundamental simplicity, were carved without distortion of features. To Stephens and Catherwood these were positive confirmation they were in the presence of the remains of a highly cultured people who could be compared with Old World civilization and yet, were entirely different. Stephens wrote:

"What we had before our eyes was grand, curious, and remarkable enough. Here were the remains of a cultivated, polished, and peculiar people, who had passed through all the stages incident to the rise and fall of nations; reached their golden age, and perished, entirely unknown.... We saw the evidences of their taste, their skill in arts, their wealth and power. There is no resemblance in these remains to those of the Egyptians; and failing here, we look elsewhere in vain. They are different from the works of any other known people, of a new order, and entirely and absolutely anomalous; they stand alone."

All the buildings discovered at Palenque are erected upon pyramidal bases. The Palace was erected around 640 A.D. and the Temple of the Inscriptions about 692 A.D. Other small temples on top of artificial platforms, and which were once plastered and painted at the time of Palenque's zenith in Late Classic times, are the Temple of the Cross, the Temple of the Foliated Cross, and the Temple of the Sun. Notable are the carved bas-relief stucco panels in their inner sanctuaries and the almost intact roof combs. Not far are the Temple of the Count, partially restored, the Aqueduct, and the remains of the North Group temple complex.

Like many other Maya sites, Palenque (300 A.D. through early 800) was not a true city but a "ceremonial centre," inhabited by priests and nobles of the ruling class. Its principal population was scattered in the countryside. Though there is not much evidence that the adjacent areas of Palenque were densely populated, it is assumed that the population had to be considerable, because of the size of the buildings and the site where construction had been going on for centuries.

The small museum is certainly worth a visit, as it houses many of the treasures found at Palenque, including pottery, jade, and stucco decorations from previous excavations—and a panel of glyphs found in the Palace. Vandals destroyed many stuccoed panels from various buildings; many others were taken out of the country by "archaeological poachers." Despite the tight vigilance of Park Rangers and border officials, this unfortunately continues. There are some panels on display in the National Museum of Anthropology in Mexico city.

Evidently the Mayas of Palenque were not involved in the "stela cult," for the visitor will not find stelas placed at key points within the ceremonial buildings, as there are in Copán and Tikal and other small sites throughout the Maya lowlands. There is no clear explanation. The customary prism-type stela common in other sites is not found here, and the only one found that resembles the others, built during the Classic period, is a figure carved in the round, which can be seen outside the museum.

The visitor will immediately experience an artistic difference: while in Copán, the artist concentrated his imagination on intricate rococo designs, in Palenque, the simple linear style was preferred by these master craftsmen. Here we do not see the Puuc style stone mosaic used in Uxmal and other sites of Yucatán; instead we see stucco everywhere. The artists almost exceeded the limits of their imagination through the ease of handling this substance.

Try to imagine how this site might have looked in its Golden Age, with its painted stuccoed carved figures, its cemented plazas, its buildings with roof combs covered with carved plaster decorations, the interiors, with their pillars and façades showing exquisite taste in depicting various ceremonial events and passages of daily life in stucco bas-relief panels, the most delicate and sophisticated of any yet found of the Maya culture.

UXMAL

Uxmal, which flourished from A.D. 600 to about 987, was first discovered by Padre Antonio de Ciudad Real in 1558 at the end of the Spanish conquest. Situated in the Puuc region of southwestern Yucatán, a range of low hills and rolling limestone ridges with some alternate pockets of soil, the dominant Classic architecture of the peninsula was founded here and lasted into the Late Classic period. Water is a problem, since the land is a shelf of porous limestone—the whole Yucatán peninsula was in prehistoric times submerged beneath the sea—and there are no subterranean rivers or cenotes as exist on the northern coast of Yucatán. The ingenuity of the inhabitants of Uxmal and the surrounding area played a decisive role in their survival: they built underground cisterns covered with a thick coat of plaster to avoid seepage.

The architecture here, in the pure Puuc Classic style, has a revolutionary technique and design different from anything seen in the rain forest of the lowlands, where constant rains challenged the Maya engineers who had to devise new ideas and techniques to protect their buildings from flooding. Some Tlaloc rain and fertility god and other supposedly foreign motifs were found at the Temple of the Magician and supposedly at the West Building of the Nunnery, though these were hardly enough to distort the pure Puuc style as happened in Chichén-Itzá. This evidence, however, does suggest some contact between the Mayas of Uxmal and the Teotihuacán culture of Mexico.

Located 50 miles south of Mérida, the Uxmal ruins cover over 250 acres. Considered to be the second best planned city after Copán, Uxmal is the largest of the Puuc sites and was ruled by the Xiu family, whose ruler is believed to have come from Mexico. There is still controversy. According to the Maya legend, the Lord Ah Suytoc Tutul Xiu was established in Uxmal about 987 A.D., and the Xiu family were apparently late arrivers in Yucatán, about the time of the Toltecs' arrival. This family seems to have quickly become strong in the area, expanding their influence toward the north, where the Cocom family had its headquarters in Mayapán. The Xius invaded and destroyed this center, killing all of the Cocom but one, who was on a trade expedition. This survivor later attacked the Xius, who had moved to the Maní area, crippling their leadership, which had reached a high level surpassing that of the

Cocom.

No longer the center of the Maya region of Yucatán, Mayapán's destruction and the constant warfare among other of its satellite cities, including some located at the lowlands of El Petén in Guatemala, meant the end of the unity of the League of Mayapán. When the Spanish arrived, the Xius allied with them in a thrust of revenge upon the Cocom, Chichén-Itzá was conquered and the last of the Cocom rulers vanished.

As allies of the Spanish, the Xius had the privilege of retaining their settlements intact, and Uxmal suffered very little other than natural decay after its abandonment by the Xius who, it is believed, moved to Mani before the destruction of Mayapán. Religion was another matter; efforts were made by the Church of Spain established at Yucatán—efforts to wipe out "pagane" beliefs.

The geographical situation of the site also helped to preserve the structures. When Stephens arrived in 1840 he was grateful for the excellent state of preservation. Catherwood, too, though sick with malaria, could not let pass the opportunity of drawing the buildings "until exhaustion." He was found that afternoon, unconscious, next to his easel. Fortunately the fever went down in the afternoon of the next day.

Catherwood insisted he was going to be all right and that there was no need to abandon the explorations at the ruins, but Stephens decided to return to New York. They arrived at Mérida where they met the kindly Don Simón Peón, friend and host, who owned the Uxmal ruins, which were part of one of his haciendas·located nearby in which Stephens and Catherwood had stayed.

Stephens and Catherwood intended to return to Uxmal, but hardships were encountered en route by boat to Havana. The captain realized they were lost; he had not used a chronometer, an essential instrument for navigation, in thirty years. After going through so much to get the drawings and impressions of the ruins, what if Stephens and Catherwood had ended in the middle of the ocean, defeated by hunger and thirst? Finally they came across an American ship, whose captain first thought them "suspicious", but took them on board anyway. The American ship did not have surplus food to share with the Spanish vessel, which at that point had no water or food. But finally water and some food was spared. Stephens and Catherwood arrived in New York on July 1839. Stephen's book, mentioned before, was completed and published in 1841. An immediate success, it was the foundation for American archaeology.

It has been said that Uxmal was the city of Maya renaissance. The visitor will notice the open and well-spaced buildings and the large plazas, which suggest that a considerable number of worshipers assembled during ceremonies. In a new method of construction, stucco was abandoned as a decoration, replaced by rubble core faced with mosaic stone with designs of geometric patterns and realistic forms of serpents, turtles, people, and masks.

Though it is sad to see so many of the matchless works of art damaged or destroyed, we are lucky to be able to admire semi-restored places like Uxmal and imagine the glory of what this city once was, evidently the residence of a highly religious and dedicated priesthood. The Mayas used copal, a resin derived from various tropical trees of the Nahuatl species as a source of incense and a base for paintings.

There were also many other wild products of the lowlands that these wise people learned to use, like medicinal plants. The bark of a tree, the Balche, called in Spanish "Pitarilla," produced an intoxicating elixir which the Mayas drank during their festivals to the point of delirium. It is strange that with all these natural contributions to their culture, they never made use of any design derived from plant life in their architecture.

Called by Thompson "The Phoenicians of Middle America," the Mayas were also skillful navigators, the only culture in Mesoamerica to use the sea as a means of communication and transportation within the entire coastal area and beyond, as well as every navigable river. Their capabilities in navigation are recorded in paintings, and they were able to reach faraway places inhabited by other Maya tribes to trade their goods. Yucatán, thanks to these capable harvesters, was the largest producer of salt in Mesoamerica. This natural commodity was the base of trade for the coastal Maya people, who had a virtual monopoly of the entire region from the coast of Campeche, the lagoons in the north of the peninsula and past Isla de Mujeres on the east.

The Stephens, Catherwood and Cabot Expedition to Chichén-Itzá

STEPHEN'S AMBITIONS did not end with the publication of his book; he wanted to revisit Uxmal and to see Chichén-Itzá. Catherwood had taken a long time to recover and had promised not to go back to the tropics, but he was also hooked, and accepted Stephens' invitation. Accompanying them was Dr. Samuel Cabot, Jr., a naturalist with an M.D. degree, who was helpful in many ways. Stephens felt he had missed too much in a paradise of bird life and wished to broaden his knowledge.

The three departed on the bark *Tennessee* October 9, 1841 and arrived at Sisal in Yucatán on October 25th. Dr. Cabot's medical knowledge opened the doors to the society of Mérida. The ancient Maya appear to have had a tendency toward squint-eyes, and deliberately increased the effect. This was considered a sign of beauty. Mothers attached small balls of a soft kind of rubberized compound between the eyebrows of their new-born babies so as to cause their eyes to squint.

The modern descendents of the ancient Maya appear to have inherited this natural tendency, which seemed to Dr. Cabot a puzzling defect. He was anxious to help, having learned a technique in Paris from the French surgeon M. Guérin. The method was to cut one of the six eye muscles which regulate the eye movement in any direction, but it was like an act of magic, a miracle, to the inhabitants of Mérida. To the point of exhaustion, Cabot operated on almost all the squint-eyed people ("biscos" in

Spanish) in the town. His achievements were warmly acclaimed and the three explorers were fêted with typically extravagant receptions.

Catherwood possessed a Daguerreotype camera, only the second ever seen in Mérida, which contributed to the success of the expedition. Before setting out for the ruins, Catherwood was able to record scenes of daily life for the archives. Stephens' literary reputation and his fame as an explorer of archaeological sites were well known, and all this publicity assured the necessary assistance for their archaeological exploration. The governor, His Excellency Don Santiago Mendez gave them all they needed.

The party reached the Uxmal ruins on November 15. Catherwood began his picture taking almost immediately, and was the first person to use the Daguerreotype extensively for archaeology. With the trained eye of an artist, he made sure nothing escaped his notice. He drew, surveyed and mapped accurately and carefully, as efficiently as before at the other ruins. Both Stephens and Cabot fell ill with malaria. Fortunately Fray Estanislao Carrillo was visiting from his Convent and was able to take care of them. Catherwood in the meantime worked very hard to finish his sketches, which he did before falling ill again himself.

Father Carrillo took care of all three explorers and as soon as they were fully recovered, in January, 1842, they continued, visiting many other small sites. Invaluable discoveries were made, and recorded in drawings and notes, but their main objective remained Chichén-Itzá, which lies on a flat plain, sixty miles from the sea. They finally reached their goal. Stephens and Catherwood registered many observations and surveys in Chichén-Itzá and wherever they explored, and these served as the point of departure for further studies by archaeologists from all over the world.

Dr. Cabot made the first ornithological surveys and collections in Central America. His exhibit of hundreds of birdskins was highly admired, especially the ocellated turkey, later made famous by Audubon. Stephens' second book, *Incidents of Travel in Yucatan* appeared in bookstores in March 1843, and its success was extraordinary. It was reprinted until the engravings were worn out; translations were made, and it is read with much interest even now.

CHICHÉN-ITZÁ and The Toltecs

CHICHÉN-ITZÁ, 75 miles from Mérida and easily reached by car, is one of the archaeological wonders of the world, covering about a six square mile area, with richly carved buildings, temples, and shrines. Many have been partially restored and some are as they were found. Much remains of mounds and vegetation. The city was first founded around 432 A.D., then abandoned after some centuries and reoccupied until the Toltecs, who also dominated most of Mexico, took over some time after 987.

With the exception of some early works found in the southern part made in the pure Puuc style, this site is less important than Uxmal for the quality of Mayan purity in its building style. This was an important town in the late Classic Maya period, and is one of the most visited Maya sites on the peninsula, lying within the zones of the arid subtropics and having a rainy season from June to December.

The Toltecs brought with them the influence of their architecture, which is seen throughout the buildings in the northern part of the city. The Ball Court, the Temple of the Jaguars, the Temple of the Warriors and its One Thousand Column Court, the Market, and El Castillo are the most dramatic ones. The Mayas, who achieved a high level of perfection in their architecture and sculpture, were also reaching their golden age as painters of frescoes and murals. Many were found in other explorations, some almost complete, such as those discovered at Bonampak in 1946. That small site contains the finest known Maya murals, painted around 800, which show us how highly technically developed they were in this art. Stephens had found vestiges of paintings of remarkable artistry and was putting things together. Inspecting the inner chamber of a temple at the north side of the Ball Court, Stephens noticed the remains of frescoes depicting Toltec life . Some of them can be seen today on the walls and ceiling.

The walls of a substructure, the Chac-Mool Temple, underneath the Temple of the Warriors were once entirely covered with frescoes in rich colors of all kinds of scenes, including body tattooing and mutilations at ceremonies, even human sacrifices. The paintings had been executed with taste and skill, the columns, jambs and pilasters were polychromed and sculptured in bas-relief. There were scenes of battle and the conquest of a village, the carrying of prisoners over the sea, boats, fishes, sea turtles, flowers, sea anemones, octopus, snails, and a human head with a protruding bar to which a small bird was attached. The latter is rare in frescoes, for it is commonly found in sculpture. There were warriors, priests and sorcerers with elaborate ceremonial staffs. There were domestic scenes, offerings, even symbols of stars and planets, identical to those found in Mexico. There were birds, faces with negroid features, and there were serpents.

The walls of the temple seem cluttered with these scenes and many more. Scenes of sea voyages showed these people were expert navigators. The paintings have not been exposed to the elements and have retained their rich original pigments. Remaining frescoes from the exterior walls of the Temple of the Warriors were also found, under 109 coats of plaster. Did the artists keep plastering the walls each time they got tired of a painting? The thickness of the coats of plaster covered even carved decorations. The frescoes were discovered by the Carnegie Institution during restoration work; all findings were recorded in a fantastic amount of work classifying every detail of every painting. It is hard to believe this temple was at one time just a pile of rubble. Before its discovery, the fragments seemed to be too much of a coincidence to Stephens. He wrote:

"For a long time we had been tentalizing with fragments of painting, giving us the strong impression that in this more perishable art these aboriginal builders had made higher attainments than in that of sculpture,...and we now had proofs that our impressions did them justice. The colours are green, yellow, red, blue, and reddish brown, the last being invariably the colour given to human flesh."

The Toltecs seem to have stimulated a last revival of Maya civilization, for the amount of work they performed seems to have been significant. The ornate elegance of the Classic Period was practically abandoned. The Toltec arts were simpler, somehow rougher—hieroglyphic texts were little used and the architectural techniques were changed, as they used columns instead of the heavy walls their ancestors had used. But the Toltec domination gave Chichén-Itzá a reputation as the most important city on the Yucatán peninsula, though they abandoned it by 1224. Where did they go?

The Itzas, despised by the Toltecs, learned that Chichén-Itzá had been abandoned, ceased their wandering and reoccupied the city. A few years later they founded Mayapán and their leader established himself there. He was Kukulkán, but no relation to the great tenth century Toltec predecessor. After his death, Mayapán became the capital of the Maya cities of the Yucatán peninsula, when another man of Itzá lineage named Cocom took over in a bloody coup.

Ruled by the Cocom until about 1461 A.D., Mayapán was attacked and destroyed by the Xiu clan from Uxmal, who later settled in Maní. The Itzá again had to wander to find their final settlement, in the jungle region of El Petén, at Lake Petén Itzá. Now known as Lake Flores, it is the island capital of El Petén province, near the Tikal ruins.

Recent excavations have further confirmed the extent of trade in the Maya world. Obsidian, not present in the Maya lowlands, was imported from the highlands and from Mexico, brought as a raw material and then shaped into working tools, including knives for animal or human sacrifices. Some consider the use of obsidian to have been a luxury, for chert, a dull-colored cryptocrystalline quartz, also known as "hornstone", present in the limestone bed of the lowlands, could very well have provided all the cutting tools necessary for the building of the Maya Empire. Still, the fine obsidian cutting edge was unsurpassed for executing such a high level of workmanship.

Non-existent in the Maya lowlands, metal was imported from as far as Costa Rica and beyond. Objects found at the Cenote or Sacred Well of Chichén-Itzá include gold artifacts from as far away as Colombia and Perú. Metal was a luxury commodity and was used less than jade, which was one of the most important materials, after obsidian, and was associated with the upper classes, found mostly in burial chambers of nobles and high priests. The list of items is long, but we have given at least a basic notion of the importance of trade in Maya life.

Of the two cenotes at Chichén-Itzá, one was used as a water supply and the other, the Sacred Well, was reserved for human sacrifices. To expiate their sins against Chac-Mool, the rain god, and in times of drought, the Mayas sacrificed women and children. In their ceremonial rites they also practiced divination about the forthcoming crops. Landa considered the Sacred Well to have been the inhabitants' most important religious shrine.

Chichén-Itzá, which was part of a hacienda, was eventually bought by Edward Thompson, an American Consul who resided in Mérida at the turn of the century. He made extensive archaeological excavations, and was the first person to use diving gear to unveil the mysteries of the Sacred Well. Vast amounts of broken pottery, human bones, gold and jade objects, and countless other lesser objects were found. They gave valuable clues about the offerings the Mayas dedicated at these ceremonies. Most of this collection is in the Peabody Museum of Harvard University.

TIKAL

FROM THE AIR, at the moment when the matted green jungle is broken, you will see towering ancient structures in the middle of nowhere. Getting off the small aircraft that brings you to Tikal from Guatemala City will be the beginning of an amazing experience. You will probably stay at the Jungle Lodge, with screen nets to protect you from insects wherever there is an open space. The roof of the whole compound is thatched and the walls of your room are independent of the roof, for better air circulation. Of course the opening is screened.

There are two other hotels, but not all rooms have private baths or hot water. A newly built campsite of limited space has thatch-roof shelters to accommodate hammocks; you may park within the boundaries if you come by car: first come, first served, and watch your belongings. Potable water is scarce, so drink soft drinks and bring halazone pills to purify local water if you decide to try it. Eventually, because of the scarcity of potable water and the danger of pollution that would result from tourist accomodation, this will be banned in Tikal and diverted to Flores. The island capital of the Department of El Petén, which surrounds Lake Petén Itzá will accommodate the tourists, and already has comfortable hotels with swimming pools, hot water and good food. Tourists are taken to the ruins in a two hour bus trip through rain forest. If you are adventurous and have a well detailed map and a guide you may walk through unmarked trails and "discover" many other ruined places.

The bird life is so exuberant that it may take you a few hours to get used to it. The communications are phenomenal, everything is said publicly and without sparing a note. Wouldn't it be interesting to know their language? The vegetation all around you is so luxuriant you wonder about your own back yard. There are orchids and flowering bromeliads. You can hear the cries of monkeys—patience and a small pair of binoculars will enable you to see them jumping from branch to branch. Bring insect repellent. There are no sounds of city life at night, just the language of the jungle. But you will be exhausted from exploring the ruins and will fall into a sound sleep.

Tikal is one of the largest and oldest of all the Maya ruins found, representing the Late Pre-Classic period until the disintegration around 900 A.D. El Petén, the northernmost province of Guatemala, is situated in the rain-forest area and was the region chosen by the Mayas to build their cities. It has enough ruins to keep archaeologists busy for centuries.

Within the boundaries of Tikal lived a population of 45,000 in Maya times, it is estimated, but still debated. After World War II, the University of Pennsylvania was engaged in a long-range program of clearing, excavating and restoring the main buildings of Tikal. Work still continues, but on a very limited basis. The Guatemalan Government has a permanent team of archaeologists working there and a crew of park rangers to protect the area, where pillaging of stelae and other objects continues. Sporadic visits and excavations by American students and archaeologists continues and the area has been declared a National Park, the largest in Central America.

The Maya civilization was colorful and spectacular.

Its rise and fall will probably continue to be a major topic of discussion for centuries among scholars, students, laymen and sightseers. Here are centers of the past where we may see many things these people accomplished without many of the utensils man has depended on in other places and times, and here and now. Did all this energy come from faith in their gods or from some other force? A constant challenge for generations of archaeologists to come, the secrets are being unveiled very slowly. We cannot even begin to visualize the stresses and strains that existed during their culture cycle, but we know that the Classic Period of about 250 A.D. to 900, was the zenith of all their ambitions, of the sciences, architecture, social life and the dynastic powers of their rulers. Why did everything stop, as if a complete silence had invaded one of our modern metropoli? Archaeologists are still searching the remains for the answer.

To the Visitor

For those interested in inspecting the remains of this extraordinary culture, Copán in Honduras and Uxmal, Palenque, and Chichén-Itzá in Mexico can be reached by car. Tikal at the moment can only be visited by air; the roads to this site are only for the adventurous driver with high axle vehicle, but eventually a modern highway will be finished. For details of your visit, consult your travel agent or the Tourist Office in each of the three countries.

The Pre-Columbian Law, overdue for a long time, has been welcomed indeed by all countries concerned with the fate of their pre-Columbian heritage. This law, passed by the U.S. Congress on October 27, 1972, grants the country of origin the sole ownership of its antiquities and also gives that country the right to decide what pre-Columbian pieces are to be sold, if any, and/or exported, and to return to the country of origin any piece that has been taken out of the country without authorization.

We hope this law will put an end to the operations of poachers and smugglers, in the past a major enterprise. The remains of a vanished culture, which left us an inheritance of the glory of its past in the magnificent pieces of art, are already scattered the world over.

THE PLATES

HIEROGLYPHIC STAIRWAY

Situated at one end of the Ball Court, this famous stairway was the leading entrance to the Temple of the Inscriptions. Thirty-three feet wide, it has sixty-three steps, each embellished on the risers with continuous inscriptions of some 2,500 separate glyphs, arranged to be read in horizontal lines rather than the conventional columns. This work resembles an encyclopedia in magnitude, unique and unsurpassed by any other Maya undertaking yet recorded. Every twelfth step there is a seated human form, whose elaborate hair dress suggests Teotihuacán influence. One is at the Peabody Museum of Harvard, whose second expedition under the direction of Dr. John G. Owens, discovered the stairway.

Archaeologists do not seem to associate these glyphs with astronomical findings, but rather to important historical events. Sylvanus G. Morley, the famous archaeologist, passed many months here studying the glyphs. The earliest deciphered date was 544 A.D. and the latest about 744. At the center of the base of this stairway is an altar with sculptured top—a gigantic serpent face in front facing the back of Stela "M". The balustrades are decorated with countless complicated designs taking the form of serpents and birds. The serpent was a deity in Maya mythology and a sign of fertility. At the front of the Hieroglyphic Stairway, Stela "M", dated 756 A.D., has glyphs recording a solar eclipse—such a prediction was an astonishing scientific achievement.

Among the offerings found at the cruciform vault were 30 pieces of pottery of diversified workmanship, some believed to have Teotihuacán influence. There were painted pieces, some jadeite, a jar filled with black sulphite of mercury covered with a conch shell, and some fragments of stalactite. "Stela" is a Greek word referring to a stone shaft set in upright position, in Maya archaeology. Stephens found this one fallen and broken, probably from earth tremors very common in this valley.

32. *COPÁN*

STELA "D"

Also situated in the center of the north side of the Great Plaza, this other unique stela has a height of 11 feet 9 inches and is dated about 736 A.D. No offerings were found in its large cruciform vault. At the back of this stela, in two parallel columns, figures of humans and animals, including fishes, parrots, eagles and frogs, are entangled with glyphs, two figures to each glyph.

The altar has two huge, grotesque, faces, one facing the stela and the other, seen here, toward the Great Plaza. This zoomorphic figure is believed to be a rain god. The ears of these figures have the form of enormous human tibiae.

Dr. John G. Owens, Director of the second Peabody Museum Expedition in 1893, is buried, according to his wish, just in front of this altar, and has my respect and admiration. His enthusiasm was so great in directing the work here that he refused to abandon his post to get medical treatment for malaria he had contracted at Lake Izabal in Guatemala—the first excavations and clearing, and the restoration of the Hieroglyphic Stairway were under way.

In Maya times, this Great Plaza was plastered and painted, presumably in the favorite color red. The entire area of this plaza is approximately 800 feet from north to south and 350 feet from east to west. The largest number of the famous four-sided carved stelae are found here, and many more scattered among the ruins and in the distant hills—the greatest number found in the whole Maya world!

The Peabody Museum began the first excavations here in 1891; the Carnegie Institution of Washington, D.C. continued in 1935 and restored most of the site as seen today. There have been no significant new excavations or restorations, but we hope increasing tourist attention will enable studies to continue. A visit to this ceremonial center is an experience of a lifetime.

34. *COPAN*

BALL COURT

This is considered to be the best representation of a Classic Period ball court. Unlike the Mexicans, the Mayas had no rings as goal markers; instead there were three stone markers in the playing alley, flat square slabs, followed by three others at the sloping walls parallel to the ones at the center. They were carved in the form of birds, serpents or other animals. Six large parrots' heads at the benches are evidently goal markers. Though Maya and Aztec rules of the game were somewhat different, both games were played with a rubber ball of oversize dimensions made from the Sapodilla tree (Achras zapota), the chicle tree.

Ball courts were usually paved of stucco. How goals were scored will remain a mystery until more hieroglyphics are deciphered. The only known records were written by early Spanish chroniclers like Landa, Torquemada, Oviedo and others, based on the Aztecs of Mexico and the inhabitants of Chichén-Itzá, showing rules to be similar to those of the Aztecs. The Maya game was called POC-TA-POC; the Aztec game was called TLACHTLI. During its explorations and restoration of 1935 to 1942 the Carnegie Institution discovered there were three superimposed courts. Court number one, at the bottom, may have been in use as early as 300 A.D. Three beautifully carved goal markers showing players facing the ball in protective postures can be seen at the Copán Museum.

At each side of the walls of the ball court is a building which once had chambers; one, almost complete, suggests they may have been used as living quarters for the players. They wore heavy shields of leather for their chests, aprons for the waist, knee pads, helmets and gloves, according to carvings, and kept the ball in motion with the hips, thighs and other parts but not the hands or calves. The losers always had to make offerings to the gods, and in many places of the Maya lowlands and Mexico and Chichén-Itzá there were bloody ceremonies where the actual bodies and heads of the losers were sacrificed. There is no evidence of this in Copán; these people may have been conservative. Though there is evidence of Teotihuacán influence, the game rules were not influenced and perhaps the bloody Teotihuacán customs were not followed. Perhaps the offerings were just valuable possessions.

Standing at the patio of the Museum at Copán is Stela 7, the oldest stela found here, fairly complete. It dates from 613 A.D. First visiting the ruins around in 1839, Stephens gave the nomenclature to most of the then visible monuments. It is still in use.

THE TORCH BEARERS

This enigmatic figure of a gigantic human kneeling on one leg and others of identical form and dimensions are found in the east and west ends of the Reviewing Stand staircase at the West Court of the Acropolis. Believed to be of non-Maya design, they have negroid features. This one has a collar of cacao-fruit beads, a serpent knotted around its waist, and a small serpent emerges from its clenched mouth. These figures hold torches with cross-like designs. This side of the court may have been designed for torch bearers to illuminate some special night ceremonies, with seats for nobles and high priests. Ten large niches above the Reviewing Stand may have been used by participants for their belongings: two are connected to what might have been a dressing chamber.

Among piles of fallen sculpture here at the West Court we find a symbol which resembles a Star of David. Here it is the Year Sign of the Teotihuacán civilization, since many sculptures throughout Copán bear Teotihuacán influence. The resemblance, however, has misled many tourists into speculation! The court, dated 771 A.D., is connected with the East Court of the Acropolis, which may once have been the most important structure of this kind at Copán. The East Court has the Jaguar Stairway, named for two huge sculptured figures standing proudly at each end, with inlaid round spots once containing obsidian disks.

At the upper wall in the center is a mask carved in very high relief, the Maya sign for the planet Venus. The ruins house countless figures of humans and animals; though interpretations vary, I believe that the artists' imaginations were at the command of the priests, who believed man and beast were once born from each other. This belief was reflected in the semihuman form with animal characteristics seen throughout their sculptures. Or these transformations of half human, half beast taking supernatural forms could be the deities of certain occasions, seasons or constellation passage. The more deities the priests ordered built the more power they had over the people, and this upheld their power of command.

38. *COPAN*

STELA "C"

This stela, in the Main Plaza at the center of its north side, is dated about 782 A.D., with a height of 13 feet. It was buried and thus protected from wind and the intense rain of the rainy season, and thus is now in excellent condition. Stephens and Catherwood found it covered by a thick layer of soil, and after it was unearthed, Catherwood made one of his most beautiful drawings. Portions of red paint, the favorite color of the Mayas can still be seen on the stela. This is the only stela of Copán that has two human figures, one at each side; on the west is a carved human face with a full beard, the only one until now recorded in the Maya world. It is at the rear of the one shown in this photograph. Glyphs are carved on its lateral sides.

The Mayas of Copán were the only ones to build cruciform vaults under the stelae; in this one remains of pottery vessels of the "flowerpot" style and other offerings were found by the Peabody Museum Expedition in 1894. The broken parts of the stela were repaired by the Carnegie Institution in 1935; some fragments of its south side inscriptions are still missing.

The imposing figures on the front and back might be dignitaries. The skillful and sensitive carving is one of the most human and beautiful designs of all. The Mayas consistently oriented important structures toward the cardinal points, and this stela was precisely placed.

Under Stela "H" were found broken pieces of collar jade and a small broken hollow gold figure—breaking may have indicated "killing" them before putting them in the chamber, probably part of the religious rituals as confirmed through many explorations. Copán is one of the most sophisticated monuments of the Maya civilization, with a high quality of organized architecture.

40. *COPAN*

THE OLD MAN OF COPAN

This gigantic stone sculpture of a human head, known as the Old Man of Copán, is dated 800 A.D. It is situated at the northern corner of the Temple of the Inscriptions, atop the Hieroglyphic Stairway, where other giant human figures are part of the decor. The southern corners of the Temple were decorated with huge stone alligator figures with their tails in upward position. Most of the sculptured figures at Copán are totally unlike those found at any other Maya site.

Copán, with its many sided steps, courtyards and plazas, could with good reason be called the step-terraced city. These stepped platforms may have served as seats for the people witnessing festivities and religious ceremonies—they were certainly spacious enough. The size of the stone blocks is tremendous and must have involved much hardship in building—labor must have been plentiful, confirming a theory that a dense population inhabited the surrounding area.

Some believe that the Old Man of Copán was once part of the cornice of the once-complete Temple 11. The area suffered a severe earthquake in December 1934, and tremors continued through 1935, when the Carnegie Institution proceeded to restore the site, sometimes of such an intensity as to tumble many monuments. Did the inhabitants in Maya times experience the same or worse, influencing them to abandon the area? During the Pleistocene Age the entire region suffered catastrophic volcanic eruptions so devastating it is doubtful any living thing could have survived. Through this entire region are found enormous deposits of tuff from that age.

42. *COPAN*

EL PALACIO—THE PALACE

> ...and through openings in the trees we saw the front of a large building richly ornamented with stuccoed figures on the pilasters, curious and elegant, with trees growing close against it, their branches entering the doors; in style and effect it was unique, extraordinary, and mournfully beautiful.

These were the first comments of Stephens in the spring of 1840, when he and Catherwood arrived at the ruins of Palenque and first saw El Palacio. They had journeyed one thousand miles through unknown land "...as wild as before the Spanish conquest..." Things have changed since Stephens' visit: El Palacio and other structures have been restored and new findings made, but practically all that Stephens put down in his records is as it was at the time of his historical visit. Through his writings and Catherwood's magnificent drawings, the world began to know and wonder about this hitherto unknown civilization.

When complete, the front of this palace had eleven pilasters covered with richly carved stucco figures at each of its outer and inner surfaces. Look for five of the remaining pilasters in Palenque today, with their carvings in fine bas-relief. You may feast your eyes on many treasures and let your imagination wander. El Palacio is a truly complicated network of buildings which includes vaulted galleries, courtyards, patios, porticoes, subterranean chambers and its four-story tower faces the four cardinal points. The tower has an interior staircase and ceilings of wooden beams, and it was used as an observation point for constellations or a simple watch-tower. Its design is uniquely Palenque, and Palenque is a unique example of an aristocratic era of Maya civilization.

El Palacio is an irregular rectangular structure of 340 feet by 240, sixty feet high, situated in the middle of the ceremonial center and all of its façades. The subterranean chambers, located beneath the southwest, are of early construction. On one of the walls of building "E", you will find an oval plaque depicting scenes from the life of the nobles of these elite quarters. Practically all the walls, porticoes, piers, friezes and any available surface suitable for bas-relief were covered with such scenes.

44. *PALENQUE*

EAST COURT OF THE PALACE

This section of the Great Palace was chosen by the nobility as one of their ceremonial points. Through all the remains of Palenque, there is not one stucco-carved panel showing an act of violence, sacrifice or self-inflicted mutilation so often portrayed in carvings and paintings found elsewhere, with the exception of Copán. The inhabitants seemed to be at ease with their rulers, who may have been wise and loved their subjects, who in turn obeyed them with a high degree of discipline. All this is indicated by the art, a magnificent expression of a peaceful and sensitive people, unmatched by that of any other of their Maya relatives at any time.

This court has doors leading into its three inner long galleries, forming a continuous passageway. Here is a sculptured panel with four figures, and on the right and opposite is another with five carved figures in stucco bas-relief. The artists who performed these masterpieces had to be highly trained, literate and having a clear perception and communication with the hierarchy, who in turn ordered these stuccoed panels depicting their social structure and special events. The artists probably enjoyed a speical place within the noble community.

The floor of this court was once paved and painted, as were all inner and open spaces connecting each building of the site. The steps were used by spectators sitting crosslegged to witness ceremonial events. To the west and in the rooms, remains of stucco figures can be seen, and at the balustrades of the lower staircase and the side walls supporting this structure are two sculptured figures.

Reminding one of those found at the Hieroglyphic Stairway of Copán are glyphs covering the outer side of the steps. The end of the corridor of this court connects with the tower of the palace and other chambers of this important building complex. To the upper right you can see a section of the fallen mansard roof which lies on top of its corbeled arches, typical of the architectural design of Palenque. The trilobate arches are also unique to Palenque.

46. *PALENQUE*

STUCCO FIGURE

On the East Court of the Palace, this noble Maya figure wearing a jade collar and bracelets evidently represents part of Maya society and is skillfully sculptured. Hanging from his waist like an apron are hieroglyphic texts. His head, as that of all Maya, is flattened, for right after birth mothers compressed their babies' heads between two boards. They also used to hang a string with a little ball between the babies' eyes to force them to become squinted. Both features were considered a sign of beauty. This carved life-size figure is an example of the fine low-relief work performed here. Instead of using stone like their relatives from Copán, these artists chose stucco, unfortunately the most perishable of all decorative techniques, especially in a rain forest.

This figure, which has been restored, did have remains of colorful paint. The Mayas developed the technique of mixing iron oxide with copal, a resin also used in incense to make color, especially red, a favorite and very long-lasting, remains of which can be seen in many buildings and stelae today. This figure has no beard—Maya mothers burned children's faces with hot cloths to prevent beard growth. The ears are pierced—children's ears were pierced to wear pendants of oversize dimensions. Mayas also painted their bodies and faces with a red color they thought pleasing, and wound a large cloth around their waist with one end falling in front, one behind. They often wore deerskin sandals.

According to Landa, the men did not eat with the women, but separately, using a mat for a table. Trade was important, and cacao and jade beads served as money. Being tattooed showed bravery. Friendships lasted long. Scenes found on sculptures and in Bonampak Murals show the upper class possessed servants, whose duties included dressing their masters in costumes and caring for them and those of their children. Chairs and stools were rarely shown: Maya preferred to sit crosslegged. Carved thrones and litters as shown in Lintel 3 of Tikal Temple IV and Lintel 2 of Temple III, were used by high priests and rulers.

48. *PALENQUE*

CORRIDOR OF EL PALACIO—THE PALACE

Some of the architectural techniques employed in large structures at Palenque are shown in the interior of this corridor or passageway leading to the west court, the observation tower court and to the interior of the palace. Mayas never achieved the true arch technique for their temples and pyramids, but they employed an arch design unique to this site and found nowhere else in the Maya world. Curiously, the trilobate arch, which can be seen in various sections of El Palacio, resembles those used in Islamic lands.

The Classic Period was a period of enthusiastic activity, when every Maya center developed its own distinctive features and specialties. Some, like Palenque, were conservative and did not permit other techniques or cultures to be introduced to distort their already established patterns of creativity. Due to the climate and weather conditions, Palenque buildings did not resemble those of Tikal and other lowland regions which were at the mercy of torrential rains from May sometimes lasting as long as August. Palenque, about thirty miles west of the lower drainage of the Usumacinta river, was not isolated from the others but its people followed a technique of their own.

Still, they loved trade; the river was a waterway inland, and with Palenque so close to the coast, there was contact with tribes along the Gulf of Mexico and the Totonac and Tajín cultures. Pottery and other artifacts reveal the influence of those cultures, which did not threaten the individuality of the art of Palenque, nor that of Tikal and Copán, where the influence of other cultures did not change the established art and building techniques. We will learn more about these inter-cultural contacts through new excavation and new findings.

Without use of the arch, the Indian builders supported their ceilings by lapping stones over as they rose, as at Ocosingo and among the Cyclopean remains in Greece and Italy, according to Stephens. The interior of the corridor and the columns were once richly carved with bas-relief stucco decorations. Remains of the cemented floor are still present.

50. *PALENQUE*

TEMPLE OF THE INSCRIPTIONS

The tomb of one of the most powerful rulers or high priests this city has ever known, around the seventh century, this fortress zealously guarded its contents for more than a thousand years. Supported by a base of nine stepped terraces, it is the highest building at Palenque, rising to a height of seventy-five feet. The center staircase, with no balustrades, is the only one that leads to the top of this symbolic temple, which in its day of glory displayed a magnificent roof comb. In the fashion of El Palacio, there are stucco decorations on the four piers supporting the roof. Scenes from the lives of rulers or high priests include a bas-relief of a noble holding a child in his arms, perhaps the same noble buried for so long in the secret chambers.

A continuous chronology of some two hundred years, one of the longest ever found, is in the inner upper chamber of this temple and has 620 hieroglyphic inscriptions. Their date is deciphered as 692 A.D. Built on raised terrain, this pyramid-temple is the only one of its kind here or anywhere else. To protect it from some of the heaviest rainfall of the Maya lowlands, Palenque was built on natural and artificial elevations, and the people used the natural water power in an ingenious water drainage system, and underground aqueduct, preventing the flooding of the site.

Their persistence and ingenuity is admirable. Though Palenque was occupied since before the Christian era, the peak of its most important achievements in architecture, sculpture and the sciences was from 610 A.D. to 783. It is believed that Palenque was one of the earliest sites of the lowlands to halt all activity, early in the 800's according to Landa.

The Maya of Palenque were not involved in the cult of building stelae like the related Maya of Copán, perhaps because the local raw material, dolomite, was more suitable for their carvings. The decorative media, stucco, a combination of fine powdered lime mixed with water, was applied in paste form to the parts of buildings to be decorated. Huge and richly decorated stuccoed structures and inner chambers rose during the peak period. The first restorations here were under the direction of Miguel Angel Fernandez on behalf of the Mexican Government, and continued later by Alberto Ruz Lhuillier.

BURIAL CHAMBER—TEMPLE OF THE INSCRIPTIONS

It is believed that divine and semi-divine ranks were given to some members of the upper classes, perhaps including the occupant of this grave. It was discovered in June 1952 by Alberto Ruz Lhuillier while performing restorations and further explorations at Palenque on behalf of the Mexican government. This was the first construction of the pyramid-temple of the Inscriptions, reached by a seventy-five-foot concealed stairway whose entrance was under a large slab with round holes plugged with stone inserts, located at the upper part of the pyramid. The purpose of these holes was to lower the heavy slab weighing several tons into place when the tomb entrance was closed by the Maya engineers. The burial chamber was a typical corbeled-vault room of about 30 by 13 feet, with a height of 22 feet.

Such divine-ranked Mayas were buried in special burial chambers with many or all of their most valuable possessions. In some cases slaves, servants or guardians were also buried within the chamber so as to accompany their master to the other world. The "divine" tenant of this tomb, sealed by a five-ton, richly carved slab around 12 feet by seven, had six young people buried outside his vault and was buried with an extraordinary rich collection of jade. About one thousand pieces were found inside his sarcophagus, in various forms and some exquisitely carved: ear plugs, pectoral bracelets, and on each finger was a great jade ring. The teeth were painted red and the body practically covered by jade ornaments.

The head was covered with a jade mosaic mask. Cement which had held the jade in place had been pulverized by time, and pieces were scattered over the sides of the skull. When the mask was restored it took the form of a human face with incredibly beautiful, skillfully executed contours. This burial mask of a "divine" ruler must have been designed and finished long before his death. Nine great figures, slightly larger than life-size, are seen here in stucco bas-relief on the walls of the tomb, positioned in succession around the walls. You may see all the findings from this burial at the National Museum of Anthropology of Mexico City.

54. *PALENQUE*

GOVERNOR'S PALACE

The Governor's Palace is the high point of a visit to Uxmal, and its imposing architecture is considered by experts to be the finest building known of the Maya world. The classic simplicity and elegant sobriety of this building and others at Uxmal is one of the most vivid experiences of a lifetime. Here is a partial view of the north side and at the far right is the Pyramid of the Magician. The Governor's Palace was one of the few buildings in a good state of preservation when Stephens arrived at Uxmal. He wrote "If it stood at this day on its grand artificial terrace in Hyde Park or the Garden of the Tuileries, it would form a new order, I do not say equaling, but not unworthy to stand side by side with the remains of Egyptian, Grecian and Roman art."

This building stands on three terraces, each a continuation of the other, of great width and length of as much as six hundred feet. The Governor's Palace stands on the third, with the principal doorway facing the range of terraces. Its facade measures three hundred and twenty feet, standing almost as perfect as when it was abandoned by its tenants. Uxmal is geographically situated away from the torrential rains that smothered so many buildings elsewhere, and from the ever-growing flora of the rain forest whose roots pulled at so many buildings of the lowlands.

The building's construction is entirely of stone, the base is plain up to the top of the doorways, and above the façade is elaborate sculpture characteristic of the Puuc style. Stephens wrote: "....the whole wears an air of architectural symmetry and grandeur; and as the stranger ascends the steps and casts a bewildered eye along its open and desolate doors, it is hard to belief that he sees before him the work of a race in whose epitaph, as written by historians, they are said to be ignorant of art and to have perished in the rudeness of savage life."

56. *UXMAL*

HOUSE OF THE TURTLES

Sculptured turtles decorating the upper façade at its cornice molding give this structure its name. This restored building is considered the gem of all the small structures of the Yucatán peninsula. The different carved designs on their backs make it seem as if the turtles are carrying messages. The purity of the building and simplicity of its decoration would suggest that it was dedicated to a special guest. To the south-west is the House of Doves, named for the dovecote decorations of its roof comb, repeated throughout the length of the façade. It has vaulted chambers almost completely decayed.

The Maya architects of Uxmal used to employ wood lintels over the doorways—the wood, that of the Sapodilla tree (Achras zapota), grows only in the rain-forest of El Petén province, three hundred miles away. The transportation of all this lumber required a great deal of manpower. Among the antiquities collected by Stephens were some notably carved lintels from the House of the Governor at Uxmal, Labná and Kabáh, and a collection of vases, figures, idols and other relics from other Maya sites. The loss of the century occurred when all these, plus Stephens' collections from Old World sites were destroyed by a fire of unknown source while on display in New York City in 1842.

Don Peón, the owner of Uxmal and a good friend of Stephens, gave him an elaborate carved death's head taken from the upper façade of the Governor's Palace, which fortunately was not at the ill-fated exhibit. Presented as a gift to Mr. John A. Cruger, sixteen stelae and the death's head were displayed, unknown to archaeologists, in his mansion on the Hudson, until discovered and acquired by the Museum of·Natural History in 1919. Now they are part of the permanent exhibit of Maya antiquities. The Museum of the American Indian, Heye Foundation, also of New York City has some pieces from Uxmal, among them two beautiful painted stucco heads.

58. *UXMAL*

TEMPLE OF THE MAGICIAN

This temple's elliptical form makes it unique. It is located at the eastern side of the Nunnery Quadrangle and has two staircases, one at the east and another at the west. The Temple of the Magician takes its name from an old Maya legend of a sorcerer hatching a child from an egg. Transformed into a dwarf in one year, the child had miraculous powers. Challenged by one of the nobles to erect a temple in one night under threat of execution, he succeeded and was named Lord of Uxmal after using his powers to accomplish other tasks.

The highest building at Uxmal, it reaches ninety-three feet. The oldest is the pyramid of the Old Woman, to the southeast of the Governor's Palace, but it is not yet restored. The Temple of the Magician was constructed in five stages, each one a temple; parts of Temple I and Temple IV can be seen at the west façade and Temples II and III lay in the interior. This pyramid-temple is one of the steepest to climb. Its architectural highlight is the unique oval shape from its bottom to its top platform.

The architecture of Uxmal is of two different styles. The Puuc is predominant; the secondary style is Rio Bec or Chenes. The latter can be seen in the decorations on the east side of the Temple of the Magician. Surprisingly, it also shows some Teotihuacán influence: the rain god Tlaloc mask and some year signs.

A recently excavated passage, running north-south, has unveiled some of the details of the mosaic stonework on Temple I. It is believed that this first temple was constructed some three hundred years prior to Temple V. The most important single sculpture found at Uxmal was at the doorway of Temple I, an exquisitely carved head of a priest or deity with tattooing on his cheeks, housed in the jaws of a serpent—now at the National Museum of Anthropology in Mexico City.

Dramatic changes were reflected in the abandonment of stela building and the use of the Long Count calendar. It seems possible that this change is closely related to mathematical calculations and celestial studies. A new culture would alleviate the burdens on the common people, who may have demanded fewer and fewer sacrifices.

60. *UXMAL*

SOUTH BUILDING OF THE NUNNERY

A quadrangle built on a high platform, the Nunnery is one of the most unusual building complexes at Uxmal. This is the South Building; at left is a north corner of the East building, with a partial view of a rain-god mask, Chac, and two zoomorphic figures, one at the upper level and one at the lower. These buildings may have been the residences of nobles and priests. The remains of four large buildings bordering a large quadrangle plaza suggest it was a ceremonial area.

Each building has a different style of decoration, probably due to construction at different times. According to George Kubler, the South Building is the second oldest here and is the entrance to the Plaza of the quadrangle through a corbeled arch portal. Eight doors face the inside of the plaza and over each are carved replicas of native houses with a rain-god mask on top. The curious placement of these decorations may have a religious meaning: perhaps the masks could call for rain, to be collected in the cisterns.

The lattice work of the upper façade and its undistinguished design suggest that it was built in a different era and for a very special religious purpose, perhaps to house a certain rank of nobility or priests. The third oldest building at the Nunnery quadrangle complex is the East Building where the decorations are in contrast to the other three. Here the architects had restrained their imagination, and it may have housed a different rank of guest; shorter than the others, this building has only five doorways. At each corner of the building are rain-god masks, with deified head figures above and below the masks.

62. *UXMAL*

CHAC—RAIN GOD—NORTH BUILDING OF THE NUNNERY

In this detail from the upper façade of the North Building of the Nunnery, famous for its rain god masks, four of them can be seen from top to bottom. These decorations were widely employed at early constructions of the Puuc Style in Uxmal and other sites as far as Chichén-Itzá and beyond. The North Building here is believed to be the oldest of the four and the longest one, approximately 270 feet. Eleven double vaulted chambers added to the others of this quadrangle total seventy-four vaulted chambers.

This site and others of the region were highly dependent on rainfall, which accounts for the presence of the rain god masks here and at other buildings of the Puuc style. The importance of religion in their lives accounted for the display of their favorite gods in important ceremonies. It is understandable that the rain god Chac was worshipped here more than any other. These carvings could be a thanksgiving for the rains received and those to come—they were marvelously carved and displayed.

This type of mask is also found at the Grand Pyramid, now under restoration, with nine platforms and an extremely wide staircase flanking the north side of the pyramid. The great rain god masks have depressions on the tops of their noses, thus differing from the other ones at Uxmal. They might have been used for burning incense as a religious offering. The largest rain mask is at the interior of the temple: its nose is eighteen inches wide, with two depressions on each side for the burning of incense.

The plentiful rain of the rainy season is collected in cisterns called *chaltunes*, large oval-shaped reservoirs holding approximately eight thousand gallons of water. This system is still employed today by the local farmers using the cisterns built by the Mayas hundreds of years ago, dug out of limestone and covered with a coat of plaster as thick as one inch.

64. *UXMAL*

WEST BUILDING—NUNNERY QUADRANGLE

This building, the latest addition to the quadrangle of the Nunnery, has richly carved mosaics of undulating serpents and seated persons with tied hands, perhaps victims for some kind of ceremony. Rich geometric designs and rain god masks different from the ones at the North Building can be seen. There may have been some foreign influence in the display of the bold and extravagant silhouettes of the serpent and the nude male figures. The façade of this building offers the greatest variety of ornamentation; it even has on its central doorway a throne with a feathered canopy. The figure on the throne has the body of a turtle and the head of an old man; this truly zoomorphic figure must have a religious symbolic meaning.

The decoration of the West Building suggests it was the residence of special guests, perhaps high-ranking priests or dignitaries. Each of the buildings faces a cardinal point, peculiar to Maya structures not only at Uxmal but throughout the entire region.

This site is much as it was in Stephens' time; because Uxmal is not situated in the rain forest, the vegetation was low and did not obstruct all the buildings, though the site is improved today. He wrote: "... to my astonishment we came at once upon a large open field strewed with mounds of ruins, and vast buildings and terraces, and pyramidal structures, grand and in good preservation, richly ornamented, without a bush to obstruct the view, in picturesque effect almost equal to the ruins of Thebes, for these, standing on the flat of the river, nowhere burst in one view upon the sight. Such was the report I made on my return to Mr. Catherwood, who lying in his hammock unwell and out of spirits, told me I was romancing; but early the next morning when we were on the ground, he commented that the reality exceeded my description."

66. *UXMAL*

EL CASTILLO

This pyramid differs from most surrounding buildings mainly because of its radial symmetry and sparse architectural sculpture. Its interior houses another small temple with a secret stairway leading to the Red Jaguar Throne Room. A life-size effigy with an open mouth was found here, painted in a mandarin red color with seventy-three circular spots of green jade including the eyes. This discovery was made by archaeologists of the Carnegie Institution of Washington D.C. in 1937 while restoring the upper temple.

A pyramid-temple and main building at Chichén-Itzá, El Castillo is in the Maya style but with Toltec decorations. It has marching jaguar carvings like the ones found at Tula ruins. Four solid staircases with an open-mouthed serpent on each balustrade, surround the four sides of the pyramid. Each staircase has 91 steps, multiplied by four staircases equals 364. The top step covering the whole quadrangular upper platform brings the number to equal the 365 days of the year. At each side of the pyramid there are nine stepped terraces divided by stairways, to make a total of eighteen sections on each side: the number of months of the Maya calendar. Fifty-two panels match the total number of years in the Calendar Round used by the Maya and presumably accepted by the Toltecs. This is peculiar to the Maya astronomy rituals recorded in their architecture.

There are two structures: the pyramid built by the Mayas was abandoned, then after a while the Itzás under Toltec domination took it over, and a new pyramid was erected over the first one. On top is a symbol of Quetzalcoatl—Kukulkán to the Mayas—the feathered serpent god, to whom it was dedicated. There are serpent columns, warriors in relief on the jambs and columns of its portico, and merlons on the roof forming a crest similar to those at Tula. It is seventy-five feet high. Richly carved Sapodilla tree wood beams were present at the interior of the upper temple as well as square columns entirely covered with elaborate sculpture.

This photograph, which was taken from the only room, the small Temple of the Jaguars facing the Main Plaza, shows a close-up of its only sculpture, a jaguar that resembles a throne. At right is one of the elaborately carved columns with Toltec decor.

68. *CHICHÉN-ITZÁ*

BALL COURT

The Ball Court elicited a profound curiosity in Stephens; it reminded him of a description of a similar court in the account of the early Spanish chronicler Herrera of the diversions of Moctezuma in Mexico City during the conquest. Stephens' accurate estimate forestalled any speculative theories as to the purpose of such unusually large parallel walls. He "expressed the opinion that they were intended for the celebration of some public games."

Four-hundred-fifty feet from north to south, this is the largest ball court found anywhere up to the present. Stephens recorded extremely detailed descriptions of the dimensions of the walls and stone rings and wrote, "on the rim and border were two sculptured entwined serpents..."

Each side of the benches (walls) has five sculptured panels; we can still see human figures with plumed headdress. Toltec-style reliefs show a triumphant player brandishing his victim's head; snakes protruding out of the loser's decapitated body represent blood. This confirms that decapitation was part of the ritual of the game during the Toltec period in Chichén-Itzá.

Made from rubber from the Sapodilla tree, the ball was struck with any part of the body except the hands. It was a great skill to hit the ball with the hips; a piece of stiff leather was fastened to the waist to improve the aim. The team that convert a goal by passing the ball through the ring at each side of the walls would win, and could claim the spectators' clothes and belongings. Although the spectators naturally tried to flee some were always caught. Then there were ceremonies of offering to the idol of the ball court: the relief panels show human sacrifices. To abolish these, the Spanish prohibited this game, to the displeasure of Moctezuma, during their occupation of Mexico City.

70. *CHICHEN—ITZA*

TEMPLE OF THE WARRIORS

This temple, a large mound at the time, was to be one more discovery for Stephens' records in 1842. While he and Catherwood were busy examining the upper part of El Castillo, stepping in and out of the platform to look down on the ruined buildings of this city, they saw for the first time groups of small columns

"...which, on examination proved to be among the most remarkable and unintelligible remains we had yet met with. They stood in rows of three, four and five abreast, many rows continuing in the same direction, when they changed and pursued another... I counted three hundred and eighty, and there were many more;... The idea at times suggested itself that they had upheld a raised walk of cement, but there were no remains visible.

While studying and clearing the area some hundred years later, the Carnegie Institution of Washington, D.C. reached the conclusion that at one time these columns supported a roof, like the one supporting the inner sanctuary of El Castillo. The serpent-like columns seen at the top of this temple are richly carved and were used to hold the lintels above the doorways. The roof of this temple, presumably of wood and stucco, has, since the site was abandoned, disintegrated. Each corner of the walls of the upper chamber has decorations of rain-god masks and the frieze of the first platform at its south side shows decoration of bears, jaguars and eagles, a combination of motifs seldom seen at other buildings of the site.

This Temple of the Warriors, which is a replica of Pyramid B found at Tula, the Toltec capital some 800 miles away near Mexico City, rises in four platforms, surpassing in grandeur the one at Tula, which was destroyed by invaders around 1168 A.D.

72. *CHICHEN—ITZA*

LA IGLESIA—THE CHURCH AT LAS MONJAS

This structure is a separated single-room temple, a satellite adjacent to the main large structure, a palace-type building which, like the one at Uxmal, is called the "Nunnery" and known in Spanish as Las Monjas. The architectural lines of La Iglesia are in the Puuc style used by the Mayas in Yucatán during late Classic times. The upper parts of this building are decorated with rain-god masks and the interior was once covered with plaster and paintings. It is said that the Indians were superstitious about this temple, saying that on Good Friday of every year they heard music or bells ringing. Stephens commented, "In this chamber we opened our Daguerreotype apparatus,—[an early type of camera] and on Good Friday were at work all day, but heard no music."

The Las Monjas building has a grand staircase fifty-six feet wide rising at the top to a height of thirty-two feet, with thirty-nine steps. At the upper platform is another staircase leading to the entrance of a decayed single chamber. The structure on top encompasses a range of buildings with a platform fourteen feet wide extending all around. On the left of the staircase are five doorways, three of which are false doors which look like recesses in the wall. The compartments between the doorways show ornaments of unusual taste and elegance. At one end the doors give access to chambers that still have paintings on their walls.

Stephens writes of chambers at each end of the building, with niches and apartments as large as forty-seven feet long and nine deep: "....all the walls from the floor to the peak of the arch had been covered with painted designs, ...the remains of which present colors in some places still bright and vivid; and among these remains detached portions of human figures continually recur, well drawn, the heads adorned with plumes of feathers, and the hands bearing shields and spears...."

This photograph is only a sample of the ornaments here.

74. *CHICHEN—ITZA*

CHAC-MOOL

This is one of the most venerated gods of Chichén-Itzá. Of Toltec origin, it was accepted by the Mayas after being introduced by the invaders. Its real name remains unknown, but Alice Le Plongeon named this rain and sun god during one of her travels to Yucatán. Her book, *Here and There in Yucatán* was published in 1886. At the upper platform of the Temple of the Warriors is this statue in reclining position with raised head. A receptacle on its stomach probably contained sacrificial offerings, including perhaps the hearts of victims.

The entrance to the only chamber of this upper structure is flanked by a pair of feathered serpents, heads and open mouths on the ground—tails straight up. At the end of this chamber and beyond these columns is a huge sanctuary, an altar supported by nineteen pygmy-like Toltec warriors. Was this altar for human sacrifices? This ritual took many forms; one of the most common was self sacrifice—offering one's own blood, mutilating parts of one's own body. Other ceremonies required the services of CHACS—the sorcerers aiding the priests—who carried out the festivals. More important were the NACOMS, called physicians; they had the responsibility of decapitation and opening the breasts of the victims, pulling out the hearts, and putting them on a plate to be given to a priest, the CHILAM, who quickly anointed the faces of the many idols for whom the victims were sacrificed. Decapitation was also practiced during the Classic Maya period, witnessed by the murals found at Bonampak, where the head of a victim rests on leaves. Another representation is shown on page 34a of the Dresden Codex. Many skulls with cervical vertebrae were also found throughout sites of the Classic period.

There was cannibalism, as the victim was divided between the lords, priests and officials. Mayas considered those who were sacrificed to be holy. Landa, who burned Maya books, knew the Mayas well and wrote in detail about their daily life.

76. *CHICHEN—ITZA*

EL CARACOL

No other building in Chichén-Itzá has such a new structural form, a combination of Toltec and Puuc styles, for Maya features such as the sky-serpent mask are seen here. Located at the center of the Puuc section of Old Chichén-Itzá, at its southern part, this building is believed to have been used as an astronomical observatory. Circular in form, it has an inner snail-like spiral stairway leading to a chamber with openings facing the four cardinal points.

At the second and principal platform is the entrance to the circular structure, which is twenty-two feet in diameter and whose top is seventy feet from the ground. Its four small doorways face the cardinal points. Stephens noticed the remains of paintings, commenting on the second level: "...the walls of both corridors were plastered and ornamented with paintings, and both were covered with triangular arch."

Some of these paintings can be seen today. It is probable that the spacious platforms supporting this building were the scene of human sacrifices which might have been related to the constellations: fourteen skulls, some with cervical vertebrae still attached, and arranged in four rows were found at one of the platforms joining the stairway, as if it was a sacrifice at the time of an eclipse or a drought.

78. *CHICHEN—ITZA*

COURT OF THE THOUSAND COLUMNS—TEMPLE OF THE WARRIORS

The Toltecs left their mark on this building. Here is a close-up of some of the columns at the west side of the front of the Temple of the Warriors, columns that caused Stephens much curiosity. They are similar to columns at the top of Pyramid B at Tula and are carved at all four sides. Stephens' discovery of these columns was the point of departure for future archaeologists: when he arrived, the area was completely covered by brush and the Temple of the Warriors in the foreground was a large mound. The Carnegie Institution cleared most of the buildings seen today.

Beneath this temple is a much earlier one known as the Chac-Mool temple with interior frescoes already described. The original color of the painted stone columns is well preserved. Four-sided sculptured columns like the ones shown here can be found at many other places of the northern part of the site. One, richly-carved and well-preserved, stands at the south side of the ball court. Stephens counted three hundred and eighty "and there were many more..."

Today we can account for only some two hundred round and square columns. At the top of each ramp, to each side, are heads of serpents surmounted by figures of standard-bearers—built to hold flags. The Temple of the Warriors was built in four platforms and originally held a roof on top of the colonnade in front of its main stairway, seen here.

80. *CHICHEN—ITZA*

TEMPLE OF THE JAGUARS

Here on the first floor is one single room, with two square columns with Toltec sculptures in low relief supporting the architrave. Dominantly overlooking the Main Plaza at the middle of these two columns is a sculpture of a jaguar with its flat back which presumably was used as a throne by Toltec leaders. This is one of the most imposing buildings of the northern section of Chichén-Itzá. The first floor, facing the Main Plaza, is of an earlier construction than the one seen here, at the top of the temple.

Throughout the entire upper frieze of this temple a repeated Toltec decoration of walking jaguars can be seen, as in Tula. Each corner of the first upper platform facing the Main Plaza houses a large serpent's head. At left, leading to the second floor, is an extremely steep stairway with balustrade carved to represent a plumed serpent. Serpents' heads are also at the upper ends of a short wide stairway leading to an upper single chamber facing the Ball Court. The stairway levels to a platform with two beautifully carved serpent columns supporting the lintels of this wide angle entrance. The door jambs also have typical Toltec carvings. In the interior are the remains of a sophisticated and colorful mural unique in the southern part of Mesoamerica. Unfortunately it has been badly defaced, but the remains tell of a battle involving hundreds of Toltec warriors in the act of capturing a Maya village. Stephens described entering: "...an inner chamber, the walls and ceiling of which are covered from the floor to the peak of the arch, with designs in paintings representing, in bright and vivid colours, human figures, battles, houses, trees, and scenes of domestic life, and conspicuous on one of the walls is a large canoe; but the first feeling of gratified surprise was followed by heavy disappointment, for the whole was mutilated and disfigured."

82. *CHICHEN—ITZA*

TEMPLE I—TEMPLE OF THE GIANT JAGUAR

This impressive and majestic pyramid-temple rises to a height of 187 feet to the top of its roof comb. Built during the Late Classic Period about 700 A.D., it is one of the most impressive of Tikal and even of the Great Plaza where it is situated, though surrounded by other important buildings and complexes. The Plaza Mayor, or Great Plaza, is the center of the city, which covers over two acres. This plaza, whose original construction started around 150 B.C., has experienced four superimpositions of plaster during a period of six hundred years. The fourth and last paving is believed to have been about 700 A.D.

Housed at the base of this pyramid and known as Burial 116 is an elaborate tomb containing a skeleton, presumably that of a high priest or noble. The tall skeleton was lying on a low stone bench dressed in ceremonial clothing , with a round conch shell on its skull. There were perforations around each edge of the shell. From each perforation hung a two-inch carved jade piece. He wore a sumptuous necklace of carved jade tubes, three to four inches long, and two necklaces of jade beads from half an inch to more than two inches in diameter, perforated at their centers.

Curiously, between the legs of the skeleton was a long, slim, jade tube with a perfectly shaped pearl at its end. Other jade pieces included bracelets, earplugs, and anklets, Also found were pottery vessels, pieces of carved alabaster and shells, and 37 bone slivers inscribed with hieroglyphic texts. There was a total of 16 pounds of jade— 180 pieces.

This finding was one of the richest of the many burial sites excavated in Tikal. One jade piece was carved in the form of a sleeping jaguar, found at Burial 196 near Pyramid II with other relics of jade, polychrome painted pottery and a variety of carved objects fit for a king. The sleeping jaguar weighs three and one half pounds and is the second largest found to date. You may see these pieces and others at the Tikal Museum.

84. *TIKAL*

TEMPLE II—TEMPLE OF THE MASKS

This massive pyramid-temple, which rises to a height of 143 feet, is also located at the Great Plaza or Plaza Mayor facing Temple I from where this photograph was taken. At its far left and right we have Temples III and IV. Temple IV is the tallest ancient standing structure of the western hemisphere, rising to a height of 229 feet. Temple II is considered to be the only Classic Period temple-pyramid in which a tomb was not found. It has been and is a challenge for treasure seekers.

Unsuccessful searches for treasure puzzled the archaeologists who directed the excavations and who were in pursuit of other spectacular hidden Maya relics. A row of stelae arranged between east and west of Temples I and II and at the front of the staircase leading to the North Acropolis is one of the highlights of this section of the Great Plaza. On the stelae are interesting carvings with dates and figures. Tikal seems to have been not only an important ceremonial center but also an administrative one, since it had such a large continuous building construction. A large population of laborers might have lived near the city limits or perhaps within, in special adjacent designated quarters, because the high-class population did not mix with laborers.

Wood of the Sapodilla tree (Achras zapota), due to its resistance against termites and climate deterioration, was used by Maya builders in major masonry. It was also used for hieroglyphic carvings. Chewing gum is even made from it! If you can climb to the top of Temple IV you will see a carved lintel, lintel 3, which, with lintel 2 from Temple III and two other carved beams from Temple I, are some of the only ancient carved ones remaining in Tikal. One from Temple II can be found at the American Museum of Natural History in New York City.

86. *TIKAL*

THE NORTH ACROPOLIS

The North Acropolis, at Plaza Mayor, a huge platform of Early Classic temples contains structures dating back to 200 B.C., but pottery found here atop bedrock dates Tikal's first inhabitants to around 600 B.C. The climax of building may have occurred between 692 A.D. and 751, continuing to 810, but none occurred after 830. The signs of decline, especially in stela construction are set at about 810, and by 889-909 the site was virtually abandoned by its rulers. The site was occupied until abound 1000 by peasants and disoriented people from the dwellings surrounding the center.

Archaeologists have dug a long deep tunnel at the back of the North Acropolis, revealing the early walls of this complex, and from the top of the Temple of the Red Stela, far right, you can get an excellent wide angle view of Temples I, II, the Central Acropolis and Temple V in the background. This platform housed fourteen pyramid-temple structures. It is at the north side of the Plaza Mayor, and access to it is through a broad stairway which stretches the full width of the plaza.

Continuous excavations at this complex of temples will reveal that Tikal perhaps was occupied much earlier than we now know. In the 1960's, the University Museum of the University of Pennsylvania found in Tikal two stone stelae with portraits of the rain fertility god Tlaloc, worshipped by the Teotihuacán people. In the early 1970's this presence of Teotihuacán influence was further confirmed when the Department of History of Art of Yale University, under the supervision of Edwin Shook, unearthed a great variety of tripod-based pottery vessels typical of Teotihuacán, decorated with scenes including young women. This evidence of Teotihuacán influence was not a threat to the purity of Classic Maya art in Tikal. The findings were similar to those made in other sites throughout El Petén province, the Maya country of Guatemala.

Tikal was first known to the scientific world in 1848, when Modesto Méndez and Ambrosio Tut first published a report on the ruins. A flood of adventurous explorers and archaeologists followed...and excavations and restorations are still in progress here.

88. *TIKAL*

CENTRAL ACROPOLIS—BALL COURT

Here in the Central Acropolis you can see and closely study several multi-story buildings, altogether forty-two structures and hundreds of vaulted rooms spread over four acres, with six courtyards—revealing one of the most ingenious architectural techniques of the Maya in Tikal. These permanent, sumptuous hierarchical residences were occupied by the nobles and high priests. At this complex, at the south end of Court 2, the largest court on the west side of the Acropolis, is the "Maler Palace," a two-storied late Classic building.

At the back of its rooms you can see the remains of what once was a huge reservoir, now overtaken by the jungle. The elite must have been in complete command of the masses as evidenced by the immense community effort in building these palatial quarters, temples and other monuments at Tikal. Landa's accounts of the Maya in Yucatán in Conquest times record that they were a peace loving people. How peaceful they were elsewhere we know only through what was left depicted in Maya carvings.

In Tikal, for instance, on Stela 10 we find an elaborately clothed individual engaged in overpowering his captive, with a war like attitude. A great variety of warfare paraphernalia is depicted on sculptures, paintings and pottery of the Late Classic Period, which seems to have been the beginning of quarrels between Maya communities.

The Central Acropolis adjacent to the south side of the Plaza Mayor has a privileged view of the main Ball Court of the three at the site, which is at one corner of Temple I, from where this photograph was taken. No goal markers have been found here, but it was assumed that the game was like games played in other nearby sites, which included a bloody ending for the losers. Temple V is not shown and is back of the Central Acropolis. Rarely visited, it has rounded corners, only one interior room, and one of the most massive stairways of any temple in Tikal. The room is the smallest atop any pyramid-temple at the site, approximately 3 feet wide and sits on top, yet on top lies the towering, massive-looking roof comb.

Three buildings at the east end of the Central Acropolis, practically at the back of Temple I, have Teotihuacán decorations, Tlaloc masks and certain other architectural peculiarities of that culture. Those in the best condition are nearest to the Mendez Causeway.

GREAT PLAZA COMPLEX

The center of the religious and ceremonial activities of the entire Maya area, believed to have covered a 25 square mile radius, was this conglomeration of buildings at the Plaza Mayor, or Great Plaza. Other buildings, not seen here, are also important, once serving as satellites to the main plaza, which was edged by several structures occupied by rulers and high priests.

This site was built on a series of natural elevated slopes which were separated by three ravines. More than 3,000 separate constructions, many of them simple dwellings, are thought to be scattered within the six-square-mile center of the ruins that have been surveyed up to the present, and an estimated 10,000 earlier structures may lie beneath. Physically one of the largest of the Central Lowland Maya cities, all of its buildings are connected by spacious causeways.

It is believed that Tikal had at least 10 deep, walled reservoirs in operation. As this site does not have a natural source of water, the people depended solely on rainfall, which in places reaches over seventy-five inches a year. Through careful planning, the Maya engineers built and paved sloped plazas and causeways, creating a sophisticated gravitation system that channeled water into paved reservoirs to prevent seepage.

In 1959, the earliest known carved stela of the site was found broken, in a refuse area. Bearing the date 292 A.D. the inscriptions are the earliest Maya hieroglyphs yet found. It uses the "Long Count" date system and can be seen in the Tikal Museum.

Tikal was officially discovered by Father Andrés de Avendaño y Loyola and his party of Franciscan companions who had left Mérida in Yucatán in a Christian Conversion Crusade to the last of the Itzá Indians, who were secluded near Lake Flores near the Tikal ruins. Then the Indians rebelled, and Father Avendaño y Loyola and his party fled and nearly perished of starvation lost in the jungle. They accidentally came across the ruins while wandering through the thick rain forest.

TEMPLE III—TEMPLE OF THE JAGUAR PRIEST

Seeing this photo, and even more by visiting this temple, one becomes aware of the power of the architectural genius of the Maya. The Temple of the Jaguar Priest reaches to a height of 178 feet and is the third tallest of Tikal. The crest of this pyramid-temple rises above the tallest trees of this jungle, dominating the surroundings, as do the other pyramids here.

The interior of the upper chambers houses the largest of all ancient carved lintels found at Tikal, covering nearly fourteen square feet. Sculptured in bas-relief, it shows a ruling noble flanked by two subjects. He stands at the front of a throne and is practically covered with jaguar skins, wearing a headdress of jaguar skins and quetzal feathers. As this scene seems to depict a priest, the temple is known as the Temple of the Jaguar Priest, from about A.D. 800.

The Mayas living in regions where this tree does not grow imported the Sapodilla tree wood from the lowlands to use in their construction. The effort cost much manpower. Looters since the first visitors have been extremely dangerous on occasion. One of the Rangers was killed in 1971 when he surprised some carrying relics out of the Park.

Maya stelae were secretly introduced into the U.S. carrying price tags of up to $350,000, but in 1972 a law was enacted prohibiting any further ransacking of these treasures, and is called the Pre-Columbian Law. Fortunately there is a lot yet to be restored at Tikal and hundreds of sites throughout El Petén and Guatemala, Yucatán in Mexico, and Honduras. Tikal was known for the finest Maya wood carvings; doorways and lintels exquisitely carved on Sapodilla wood were found here, but the first and best was carried away by a Swiss to a Swiss museum, and the others followed. Practically the only ones left are the ones described earlier, which would collapse if anyone tried to take them, for the action of time has weakened them so much.